STANDBY TO STANDBY

WHY *YOUR* VETERAN BENEFITS ARE TAKING SO LONG AND *WHAT YOU* CAN DO ABOUT IT

WADE B. COYE

ATTORNEY / AUTHOR / VETERAN

COYE LAW FIRM

730 Vassar St, Suite 300
Orlando, FL 32804

407-648-4940
866-Wade-Coye

COYELAW.COM

Design and publishing by:
Word Association Publishers
205 Fifth Avenue
Tarentum, Pennsylvania 15084

www.wordassociation.com
1.800.827.7903

TABLE OF CONTENTS:

A WORD FROM THE AUTHOR:

Most veterans remember the immortal words "keep your paperwork squared away" when they separated from their unit. Even in our digital age, it's the paperwork and supporting documents that can delay or cause the complete loss of benefits that you as a veteran or family member have earned because of military service in the Armed Forces of the United States of America. We live in a great country with unlimited opportunities and freedoms that are hard-fought. Yet, no system is perfect, and this book, like the last, was made because it is an imperfect system and oftentimes veterans are lost and unsure of where to turn. Digital systems have streamlined things so they are better than ever, yet they still take ridiculous amounts of time. I have repeated below much of what I wrote for the first edition because what was relevant five years ago in 2017 remains today, even with substantial improvements in the system.

Listen up! If you are reading this, you're probably one of the hundreds of thousands of veterans currently struggling with the Veterans Administration, an organization that moves about as quickly as a slug through honey. Luckily for you, you've made the right decision by picking up this book. I've spent decades working with people in situations not unlike yours, and I know what it takes to build a convincing case for you.

You've served your country, but now your service-connected injuries or illness have made it difficult for you to transition to civilian life. The law moves slowly, and science continues to give us more insight into how exposure to various environments, combat, and training can cause life-changing problems. More than ever, there is an increasing awareness that exposure to a host of chemicals and other substances in the rear and on the battlefield has caused and or contributed to a multitude of medical issues that need treatment and compensation.

Unfortunately, applying for these benefits and navigating the system on your own is frustrating. A weak or incomplete claim could stall for a long period of time before ultimately being denied.

As a veteran myself, father of a Marine, and a lawyer for over 30 years who has helped hundreds of veterans with their disability claims, I know firsthand many of the problems and perils of the system. While it is easy to rail against a bureaucracy, there are people who work for the Veterans Administration who genuinely care for the veterans it serves. Unfortunately, the size of the organization means there are problems that require expert lawyers to solve. This book will help you understand the basics of veteran disability claims, as well as offer some tips and helpful suggestions. The better you understand the system, the quicker you can receive the benefits you deserve.

Best of luck with your claim!
Wade B. Coye

THE MATERIALS AVAILABLE IN THIS PUBLICATION ...

are for informational purposes only, and not for the purpose of providing legal advice. You should contact your attorney to obtain advice with respect to any particular issue or problem. Use of and access to this does not create an attorney-client relationship between Coye Law Firm, Wade Coye, or other lawyers at his law firm and the user or reader.

YOU HAVEN'T APPLIED YET? WHAT HAPPENED TO 15 MINUTES PRIOR!?

CHAPTER ONE

HAVEN'T APPLIED YET?

Applying for VA benefits is complicated, time-consuming, and fraught with peril. The system is forgiving for mistakes, but the time it takes can be daunting. Many veterans find that they need someone to help them, a family member or close friend, or, in our case, a legal team that has deep background and experience with the various disability systems in the United States.

The Department of Veterans Affairs website states, "If you have a service-related disability and you were discharged under other than dishonorable conditions you can receive benefits for your disability." Therefore, as long as you have sustained or developed a disabling injury or condition, or had a pre-existing condition aggravated while on active duty, then you are eligible for benefits and compensation. One of the biggest changes that have occurred is the substantial number of illnesses where there is a presumption of connection to military service. This has eliminated the need to undergo a painstaking process of proving a connection between certain illnesses and military service.

I distinctly remember my uncle, who was diagnosed with Parkinson's disease many years after his service in the jungles of Vietnam as an infantry soldier. It was a devastating diagnosis for him and his family. Yet, despite years of evidence of exposure to Agent Orange, a known carcinogen that creates numerous diseases, he was told he needed to "prove" that during his time in the infantry, he was exposed to Agent Orange. He was understandably incredulous, since he and other veterans pointed out that it was sprayed by airplanes and dripped from the trees.

Veterans of all backgrounds can apply, regardless of service length, which war they served in, and whether they were involved in combat or not. If you have not applied to the VA yet, you should do so right away. It's easier than ever, so please do it now.

I understand it can be a daunting process, but that's why I wrote this book; to help veterans and their families navigate the system. The pages of this book are just a start and are not in any way intended to be a full-on course of study. Your starting point should be to register on va.gov. It is available to all veterans and has improved over the past several years. I have included some basic help areas below, but if you are experiencing some problems, you can always call someone on my team to help walk you through this essential start.

CHAPTER TWO

WHAT IS THE "VA?"

The VA stands for Veterans Administration and, according to the VA website, its mission is to "fulfill President Lincoln's promise 'To care for him who shall have borne the battle, and for his widow, and his orphan' by serving and honoring the men and women who are America's veterans."

Before the civil war even ended, President Lincoln ,together with Congress passed a law creating a place for wounded veterans to receive badly needed medical care. Since Lincoln's presidency, the Veterans Administration has greatly expanded.

The important thing to remember about all this is the VA was created to help YOU. Although the different restrictions and forms can be overwhelming or confusing at times, remember that you have a right to these benefits, no matter how challenging it may be to obtain them. Veterans have had to continue to fight for benefits after fighting America's wars. For instance, after World War I Congress enacted new legislation designed to assist veterans with disability compensation, health benefits, training, and hospitals and ordered the creation of Federal agencies to administer the needed benefits.

President Ronald Reagan elevated the Veterans Administration to a cabinet-level post, demonstrating the nation's commitment to those who have served in the military and who have medical, disability, and other needs resulting from their service to the country.

If you are applying for benefits, you will deal with the sub-branch of the VA known as the Veterans Benefits Administration, or the VBA. The goal of this organization is to provide veterans with the benefits they deserve for conditions that prevent them from working and to get them the treatment they need to be healthy. Of course, if you are already familiar with the VBA or VA, you know this isn't always the case.

Frequent changes are made to streamline the process, but those changes are poorly understood and communicated. The VA is also incredibly overwhelmed with the number of cases due to funding and staffing issues. This combination confuses Veterans applying on their own, who often find themselves lost in the system. In fact, only 5% of veterans receive benefits every year who apply.

My goal is to break down the VBA benefits application process and help you, someone who served our country, get the benefits you need and deserve.

BENEFITS AVAILABLE TO VETERANS

Here is a brief list of benefits available to veterans. This is by no means an exhaustive list.

- Health Care
- Reimbursement of travel costs
- Counseling
- Maternity Care
- VA Pension
- Aid and Attendance and Housebound Benefits

- OEF/OIF/OND Care Management
- Home Improvements
- Services for Blind or Visually Impaired Veterans
- Mental Health Care Treatment
- Veterans Crisis Line
- Outpatient Dental Treatment
- Vocational and Work Assistance Programs
- Long-term Care Services (nursing home care)
- Emergency Medical Care in U.S. Non-VA Facilities
- Foreign Medical Program
- Caregiver Programs and Services
- Disability Compensation
- Concurrent Retirement and Disability Pay (CRDP)
- Education and Training:
- Post-9/11 GI Bill®
- Marine Gunnery Sergeant John David Fry Scholarship Eligibility
- Home Loan Guaranty:
- VA Acquired Property Sales
- Loans for Native American Veterans
- VA Life Insurance
- Traumatic Injury Protection
- Family Servicemembers' Group Life Insurance Coverage
- Accelerated Death Benefits
- Service-Disabled Veterans Insurance
- Veterans' Mortgage Life Insurance
- Free admission to national parks and federal recreational lands (visit nps.gov for more information.)

- Housing Grants for Disabled Veterans

- Specially Adapted Housing Grant

- Temporary Residence Adaptation

- Vocational Rehabilitation and Employment

- Chapter 36 Education and Career Counseling

- Health Care for Reentry Veterans Program

- Veterans Justice Outreach (VJO) Program

- Transition Assistance Program

- State Employment Services

- VA Health Care for Homeless Veterans (HCHV) Program

- Homeless Veterans Supported Employment Program

- VA's Homeless Providers Grant and Per Diem Program:

- VA Benefits for Veterans Living Overseas

- Unemployment Compensation

- Dependents and Survivors Health Care

- Veterans Mortgagees and favorable rates and down payments. Including multi-family housing. (the no money down program)

CHAPTER THREE

DO YOU QUALIFY?

To qualify for veteran's disability compensation benefits, a veteran must:

- Have a disabling injury or condition related to active duty service in the military

- Have a disabling injury or condition that was made worse as a result of military service.

- Have been discharged under conditions that were not dishonorable

You may be awarded more benefits if you have:

- A severe disability

- Lost a limb

- A spouse

- A child or children

- Dependent parents

- A disabled spouse

DIRECT SERVICE-CONNECTED DISABILITY

The most common VA disability application is for a service-connected disability. According to the code of federal code of regulations, it is defined as:

> "Service connection connotes many factors but basically it means that the facts, shown by evidence, establish that a particular injury or disease resulting in disability was incurred coincident with service in the Armed Forces, or if preexisting such service, was aggravated therein."

This is a pretty self-explanatory title: If you now suffer from an injury or chronic condition because of your service, you can apply for benefits because of that condition. For your condition to qualify, the VA must provide clear and unmistakable evidence your condition didn't exist prior to your service. Do you remember those days when you first reported to the recruitment station and were transported to another destination known as MEPS (Military Entrance Processing Station)? Well, this is where it starts. If you had a medical problem that was either noted during the exam or overlooked, it can greatly impact your ability to receive benefits in the future. Most problems start with a lack of documentation that a problem was caused by something.

It's important to note that Direct Service Connection is not presumptive, meaning that a link (or nexus) between the condition and an in-service incident must be proven. Evidence to prove this fact can come from medical opinions, service records, and Disability Benefits Questionnaires. I will go into detail on this in the section on C&P exams.

PRESUMPTIVE ILLNESSES AND CONDITIONS

A presumptive illness is a condition the VA presumes was caused by your military service under specific conditions. By law, the VA does not require you to prove they are service-connected– only that you meet specific service requirements. This is important because many service-linked conditions may manifest months or years after the fact, which can make proving that link much more difficult. The inclusion of more toxic exposure-related conditions is a massive step toward providing Veterans with the benefits they need and deserve. These illnesses almost guarantee significant benefits, so knowing if you qualify is important as you prepare to submit your claim.

Presumptive illnesses and conditions can change as lawsuits and new research reveal new illnesses which were directly impacted by VA service. The most recent expansion of VA benefits occurred in August 2022 with the PACT Act.

This new expansion of VA Disability Benefits is the largest in VA history. It greatly benefits Veterans who served in the Gulf War, Vietnam War, and Post-9/11 eras by further recognizing presumptive conditions based on toxic exposure while in service. Presumptive conditions save an immense amount of time and energy when filing a claim.

As you begin the claim process, it is important to keep abreast of changing developments with veterans' disabilities. Because of the complexity, there are numerous lawsuits ongoing in many different areas that could impact your particular case. In this book, we will be reviewing up to date VA legislation to get the benefits you are owed.

What Conditions are "Presumed"?

How to find out if you qualify.

Note that it is not a complete or comprehensive list of presumed conditions. If you don"t qualify under the conditions stated here, you may still qualify, don't give up!

FORMER PRISONERS OF WAR
- Imprisoned for any length of time and disability at least 10% disability rating
- Imprisoned for at least 30 days, and at least 10% disability rating

VIETNAM VETERANS
Exposed to Agent Orange
- Served in the Republic of Vietnam between 01/09/1962 and 05/07/1975

ATOMIC VETERANS
Exposed to Ionizing Radiation
- Participated in atmospheric nuclear testing: occupied or was a POW in Hiroshima or Nagasaki

GULF WAR VETERANS
Undiagnosed Illness
- Served in the Southwest Asia Theater of operations during the Gulf War with a condition of at least 10%

BURN PITS

A common way to dispose of trash in overseas military sites, burn pits exposed veterans to hazardous gasses such as plastics, chemical mixtures, and medical waste burned in the trash pits.

As I previously mentioned, the PACT Act was the largest expansion of VA Disability Benefits in VA history. These presumptive conditions were added due to Veteran exposure to burn pits and other toxic exposures during the Gulf War and Post-9/11 eras. It was the main focus of the act to expand the benefits for Veterans who were exposed to hazardous materials in this era.

Below, you will find the qualifying conditions and the service requirements to see if you qualify.

- Brain Cancer
- Gastrointestinal Cancer of any type
- Glioblastoma
- Head Cancer of any type
- Kidney Cancer
- Lymphatic Cancer of any type
- Lymphoma of any type
- Melanoma
- Neck Cancer
- Pancreatic Cancer
- Chronic Obstructive Pulmonary Disease (COPD)
- Chronic Rhinitis
- Chronic Sinusitis
- Constrictive Bronchiolitis or Obliterative Bronchiolitis
- Emphysema
- Granulomatous Disease
- Interstitial Lung Disease (ILD)
- Pleuritis

- Reproductive Cancer of any type
- Respiratory (breathing-related) Cancer of any type
- Asthma that was diagnosed after service
- Chronic Bronchitis
- Pulmonary Fibrosis
- Sarcoidosis

Service Requirements for these conditions are as follows:

You must have served on or after September 11, 2001, in any of these locations:

- Afghanistan
- Djibouti
- Egypt
- Jordan
- Lebanon
- Syria
- Uzbekistan
- Yemen
- The airspace above any of these locations

Or, on or after August 2, 1990, in any of these locations:

- Bahrain
- Iraq
- Kuwait
- Oman
- Qatar
- Saudi Arabia
- Somalia
- The United Arab Emirates (UAE)
- The airspace above any of these locations

I need to caution you that this list continues to grow. Different military environments cause different problems and we are continuing to learn about how exposure to various toxic chemicals and products can cause significant health problems for many people. The sad part is oftentimes we don't discover the harm until after a person has been exposed. Sometimes the research takes years, and then the government is slow to be on top of the evolving information.

AGENT ORANGE

From 1962-1971, the U.S. military used Agent Orange in Operation Ranch Hand during the Vietnam War. This herbicide used a chemical contaminant known as Dioxin which is now known to cause birth defects, cancers, diabetes, and a variety of other disabilities. While the U.S. military no longer uses Agent Orange, its impact is still felt by those exposed to the hazardous chemical and are now suffering from its effects.

Because of the amount of evidence connecting certain disabilities to Agent Orange exposure, the VA does not require you to prove your illness started or got worse because of your military service. Instead, you must meet the following requirements.

According to the VA Agent Orange site, a presumptive illness is added "when sound medical and scientific evidence" shows a connection between agent orange and an illness.

- Bladder Cancer
- Chronic B- Cell Leukemia
- Hodgkin's Disease
- Some soft tissue sarcomas
- AL Amyloidosis
- Chloracne

- Multiple Myeloma
- Non-Hodgkin's Lymphoma
- Diabetes Mellitus type 2
- Hypothyroidism
- Ischemic Heart Disease
- Parkinsonism
- Parkinson's Disease
- Prostate cancer
- Respiratory Cancers
- Peripheral neuropathy, early onset
- Porphyria Cutanea Tarda
- High blood pressure (also called hypertension)
- Monoclonal gammopathy of undetermined significance (MGUS)

To receive benefits based on these conditions, you also must have served any length of time in at least one of the following locations from January 9, 1962, and May 7, 1975.

- In the Republic of Vietnam or on the waterways on a U.S. Military Vessel
- Served on a U.S. military vessel 12 nautical miles or less on the waters of Vietnam and Cambodia
- Served on the Thailand U.S. Army base or Royal Thai Air Force bases
- Any U.S. or Royal Thai military base in Thailand from January 9, 1962, through June 30, 1976
- Laos from December 1, 1965, through September 30, 1969

- Cambodia at Mimot or Krek, Kampong Cham Province from April 16, 1969, through April 30, 1969

- Guam or American Samoa or in the territorial waters off of Guam or American Samoa from January 9, 1962, through July 30, 1980

- Johnston Atoll or on a ship that was called at Johnston Atoll from January 1, 1972, through September 30, 1977

- Had repeated contact with a C-123 aircraft where Agent Orange was assigned

- Had repeated Contact with Agent Orange during service for its transport, testing, storing or other uses

Certain Reserve Officers at specific locations may also be eligible for benefits.

CAMP LEJEUNE

If you served on Camp Lejeune military base between August 1, 1952, and December 31, 1987, you may be eligible for presumptive disability due to exposure to hazardous chemicals in the drinking water. According to the Camp Lejeune Justice Act of 2021, you may also be allowed to sue and recover damages from the U.S. government.

Now, remember how I talked about staying up to date with VA lawsuits and cases as you apply? Camp Lejeune is a great example of why! As of August 2022, there is a massive lawsuit all across America for veterans who were exposed to the hazardous drinking water at Camp Lejeune. Already this lawsuit has impacted legislation. The PACT Act alone has the Camp Lejeune Justice Act to help veterans affected. It's in your best interest to follow this lawsuit to see if you can qualify for new Presumptive Illnesses in Camp Lejeune.

As of this book's publication, conditions include the following,

- Adult Leukemia
- Aplastic Anemia and other myelodysplastic syndromes
- Bladder Cancer
- Kidney Cancer
- Liver Cancer
- Multiple Myeloma
- Non-Hodgkin's Lymphoma
- Parkinson's Disease

You also must have served at Camp Lejeune or MCAS New River from August 1953- December 1987 for at least 30 consecutive days.

IMPORTANT: Remember the PACT Act? It included the Camp Lejeune Justice Act. This legislation expanded screening and treatment services for exposed veterans. More urgently, it required veterans to apply for compensation within two years of the bill's enactment. Therefore, <u>you may not be eligible for Camp Lejeune benefits past August 2024. If you wish to pursue money for exposure at Camp Lejeune, do not wait, you must contact an attorney immediately.</u>

EXPOSURE CASES

An exposure case is a situation where during your military service, you came in contact with some type of substance and as a result contracted a disease and or medical condition that is impactful to you and your family. What has changed significantly are a number of situations where there is a presumption that either you were exposed, or that your exposure has caused or contributed to an illness or disease. It is most complicated and if you have developed some medical issue and served in the military it is very important for you to investigate whether your medical issue should possibly entitle you to military benefits. Sometimes called "presumption of exposure," these cases can afford you significant benefits if you have been exposed to the following harmful materials. You should know that even if there is not a "presumption" it can be possible with the proper documentation including testimony to establish a military connection to a problem. Additionally, some of the exposure issues are not as common today, some were quite impactful on military veterans of past wars, and newer exposures impact veterans who have served more recently. I have attempted to list many of the common exposures below.

ASBESTOS

Once a common building material, Asbestos has now been found to release toxic chemicals when damaged. Now the VA offers presumptive care if you were exposed to Asbestos while in service. To qualify for Asbestos exposure, you must have worked in one of these fields:

- Mining
- Milling
- Shipyards
- Carpentry
- Demolition
- Construction

Or worked with products such as:

- Flooring
- Roofing
- Cement sheet
- Pipes
- Insulation
- Clutch facings and brake linings (called friction products)

If you have worked with any of these materials or worked in any of these fields, ask your doctor about getting tested for lung illnesses. The VA can review your case for asbestos exposure.

MUSTARD GAS OR LEWISITE

Mustard gas was a dangerous chemical weapon commonly used in WWI, WWII, and the Iran- Iraq War during the 1980s. The military also used veterans for extensive testing of Mustard Gas side effects between 1942 and 1975. This research impacted as many as 60,000 veterans.

Mustard Gas notably contains an organic compound known as Lewisite, which contains Arsenic. Exposure to Arsenic can cause cancers, cardiovascular disease, and neuropathy.

If you think you've been exposed to Mustard Gas, talk with your local VA Environmental Health Coordinator to see if you are eligible for disability benefits.

GULF WAR ILLNESS

Veterans of the Persian Gulf War of 1990-1991 may suffer from a variety of chronic and acute conditions. Among these are cognitive issues, fibromyalgia, cardiovascular disease, musculoskeletal pain, and dyspepsia. This cluster of symptoms has come to be called Gulf War Illness, or Desert Storm Disease. The cause of this affliction is subject to debate, and research is inconclusive as to whether it is a result of toxic exposure, microbiological exposure, or psychological factors. Though we can't be sure yet of what causes Gulf War Illness, the VA currently recognizes it as a service-linked condition for veterans who served in one of two time periods:

Gulf War Illness Linked to Southwest Asia Service
If you served in the following areas:

- Iraq, Kuwait, Saudi Arabia
- The neutral zone between Iraq and Saudi Arabia
- Bahrain, Qatar, and the United Arab Emirates (U.A.E.)
- Oman
- The Gulf of Aden and the Gulf of Oman
- The waters of the Persian Gulf, the Arabian Sea, and the Red Sea
- The airspace above any of these locations

You must also meet the following eligibility requirements.

You must have been diagnosed on active duty OR before December 31, 2021. You must also be ill for at least 6 months and have a disability rating of 10% or higher. As you may have concluded by now, sometimes you need to pursue other disabilities first in order to qualify for additional benefits. You then qualify if you have one of the presumptive diseases:

- Functional gastrointestinal disorders
- Chronic Fatigue Syndrome
- Fibromyalgia
- Other undiagnosed illnesses, including but not limited to cardiovascular disease, muscle or joint pain, and headaches

If you did not receive a diagnosis until over a year after your date of separation, you can still qualify if you receive a disability rating of 10% or higher for one or more of the conditions listed below:

- Brucellosis
- Campylobacter Jejuni
- Coxiella Burnetii (Q fever)
- Nontyphoid Salmonella
- Shigella
- West Nile virus
- Malaria

Furthermore, you may receive benefits if you were diagnosed with the following conditions anytime after you leave service.

- Mycobacterium Tuberculosis
- Visceral Leishmaniasis

Gulf War Illnesses Linked to Afghanistan Service
To qualify for benefits for Gulf War Illness linked to Afghanistan Service, you must have started active duty on September 19, 2001, and have an illness or condition rated at 10% or more.

You may qualify for the following conditions if you were diagnosed within one of your dates of separation.

- Brucellosis
- Campylobacter Jejuni
- Coxiella Burnetii (Q fever)
- Malaria (or sooner in some cases)
- Nontyphoid Salmonella
- Shigella
- West Nile Virus

You may qualify for benefits if you were diagnosed with the following conditions anytime after your date of separation.

- Mycobacterium Tuberculosis
- Visceral Leishmaniasis

The important thing to remember is the rules do change, science catches up and helps identify causes or partial causes of illnesses. Keeping on top of the changes is important in the pursuit of VA benefits.

PROJECT 112/SHAD

Project 112 and Project SHAD were Department of Defense test programs in Fort Douglas, Utah. Roughly 6,000 service members were involved in these tests which included biological warfare testing. If you participated in these tests, the VA should have sent you a letter informing you of possible risks and health concerns. If you have not received a letter but did participate in the projects, call the VA at 1-800-749-8387.

Currently, the VA does not recognize any long-term health issues related to involvement in Project 112/SHAD, and reviews disability ratings on a case-by-case basis.

RADIATION

The VA recognizes most types of Cancer are the result of radiation exposure. Therefore, if a veteran now suffers from one of the following conditions, they may be eligible for benefits. Radiation exposure can occur in a number of situations including work with nuclear weapons, cleanup duties on bases holding nuclear weapons, service on ships and submarines that have nuclear power plants, providing repair services on those reactors, and so on. The list is not by any means limited. However, you should know that it is incumbent upon the service member to prove the exposure.

- All forms of Leukemia except Chronic Lymphatic (lymphocytic) Leukemia
- Thyroid Cancer
- Breast Cancer
- Lung Cancer
- Bone Cancer
- Liver Cancer
- Multiple Myeloma
- Posterior Subcapsular Cataracts
- Non-malignant thyroid nodular disease
- Ovarian Cancer
- Parathyroid Adenoma

- Skin Cancer
- Esophageal Cancer
- Stomach Cancer
- Colon Cancer
- Pancreatic Cancer
- Kidney Cancer
- Urinary Bladder Cancer
- Salivary Gland Cancer
- Tumors of the brain and central nervous system
- Cancer of the rectum
- Lymphomas other than Hodgkin's Disease
- Prostate Cancer
- Any other Cancer

And you must have had contact with ionizing radiation in one of these ways while serving in the military:

- You were part of atmospheric nuclear weapons testing,
- You served in the postwar occupation of Hiroshima or Nagasaki,
- You were a prisoner of war (POW) in Japan,
- You worked as an x-ray technician, in a reactor plant, or in nuclear medicine or radiography (while on active duty or during active or inactive duty for training in the Reserves),
- You did tasks like those of a Department of Energy (DOE) employee that made them a member of the Special Exposure Cohort (See 42 U.S.C. 7384L(14))

You may also qualify for disability benefits if you served in at least one of these locations and capacities:

- You were part of underground nuclear weapons testing at Amchitka Island, Alaska,

- You were assigned to a gaseous diffusion plant at Paducah, Kentucky,

- You were assigned to a gaseous diffusion plant at Portsmouth, Ohio,

- You were assigned to a gaseous diffusion plant at Area K-25 at Oak Ridge, Tennessee

SECONDARY CONDITIONS

Secondary conditions are not a direct result of service; however, they form as a result of primary conditions. It is defined in the Code of Federal Regulations as:

> "disability which is proximately due to or the result of a <u>service-connected</u> disease or injury shall be service connected. When service connection is thus established for a secondary condition, the secondary condition shall be considered a part of the original condition."

If you were to injure your knee overseas, for example, and the resulting limp causes cramps and hip pain, then the knee injury is a primary condition and the cramps/hip pain are secondary condition. When you apply for VA disability benefits, it's crucial to consider not just the initial issue, but also any other issues that can be traced back to it.

Claims relating to secondary conditions require evidence of causation– medical proof a non- service-related issue is caused or worsened by a service-related one. One of the best ways to go about this is to get a nexus letter from your doctor–something we'll discuss in more detail later in the book. Just remember, it's not uncommon for someone to develop additional leg problems if they had an injury to their foot, ankle, knee, or hip.

It is vital you conduct research on your primary conditions and see if you are eligible for secondary condition benefits. These conditions change frequently.

PRE-EXISTING AGGRAVATED CONDITIONS

If you have a condition that existed before your service, you still may be eligible to receive benefits for the condition by proving it was aggravated by your time in service.

As a veteran, I know the challenging conditions you faced during your time in service: harsh weather, long hours, and grueling physical work are all difficult even for the healthiest of people. If you had a previous condition, this work environment can aggravate your injury or illness. The VA knows this and allows veterans to apply for benefits for pre-existing conditions if they can prove an incident or environment aggravated it. The Code of Federal Regulation defines "aggravation" as,

> "a preexisting injury or disease will be considered to have been 'aggravated' by active service 'where there is an increase in disability during such service,' unless the increase is due to the natural progress of the disease."

As for how the VA determines if your service aggravated your condition, it will consider what your duties were in service, the environment they served, and how your symptoms have increased in severity.

The most common example of this is flat feet. This is when the arch of your foot collapses, causing pain and instability when walking. If you had flat feet before service, your condition may have worsened with excessive walking and poor footwear.

Before you entered service, you underwent a Service Induction Examination which listed any conditions you had before entering service. It is important you have a record of this examination in your file when you apply.

The key to receiving benefits for a pre-existing condition is to receive a medical opinion testifying your health has worsened because of your service.

CHAPTER FOUR

THE EASIEST WAY TO GET MONEY FROM THE VA!

Once you've decided to apply for benefits, it's in your best interest to become familiar with the VA online ebenefits system. The online system is a fast and easy way to apply for benefits, check your claim status, and upload evidence to support your claim.

HOW TO CREATE AN EBENEFITS ACCOUNT

A DS Logon Premium account is a VA ebenefits account that will allow you to submit a claim, upload claim evidence, and review your claim status. These useful features will expedite your claim process significantly and keep your claim organized for both the VA and you.

STEP 1: First, go to https://www.va.gov/sign-in/. You should see four login options: Login.gov, ID.me, DS Logon, and My HealtheVet. All of these could be useful accounts, but a DS Logon is the most necessary.

STEP 2: You should then be redirected to the VA My Access webpage. On the bottom of the page, there should be a "Need an Account" button. Click this to get started.

STEP 3: Another page should appear. At the top of the page is the text explaining that by selecting an option and continuing, you will begin a 10-step process to create a DS Logon account. Select the option that applies to you and continue. Depending on the option you pick, your registration process will vary. If you select registration through your "Common Access Card (CAC)," you will automatically have access to your ebenefits account. If you select registration by manual information, enter the information required. Continue to follow the instructions below.

STEP 4: Select no to both the DFAS myPay account and to have a DS Logon. They both are unreliable methods to create an ebenefits account and may delay the process.

STEP 5: Click to register and apply for a Level 1 eBenefits Basic Registration account. Then, fill out the information asked.

STEP 6: Finally, to upgrade your Level 1 account to a premium account, complete the "Remote Proofing Process."

STEP 7: Enjoy the benefits of having a premium eBenefits account!

NOTE: If you continue to struggle to make an online account, call the VA Health Benefits number at (877)222-8387. You can also call my office (407-648-4940) and my team is happy to help you get started. As with many things on the internet, the sites are updated regularly and improvements are part of that process, albeit some improvements some-times don't feel like steps forward. Nevertheless, keeping an eye on your account is important. Government websites are more consumer-friendly and provide meaningful informa-tion about your benefits.

CHAPTER FIVE

HOW DO I GET BENEFITS?

The VA has different application systems depending on the type of claim you are submitting. This section will explain the types of applications you may need to submit and how to submit them.

As of March 24, 2015, you <u>must</u> submit a formal claim for your benefits by submitting the Veteran's Application for Disability, Compensation, and Related Compensation benefits also known as of the date of this book as VA Form 21-526EZ. In order to receive additional benefits for family members, include the appropriate marriage certificates, birth certificates, and doctor's reports with your application. Please remember that the publishing date of this book in some cases can make reference to forms and websites out of date by the time you are reading this. The point is, to get your account

Photo Courtesy of Adoratia Purdy

(CC by 2.0)

familiar with the various rules and forms and regulations to move your claim along as best possible.

As with any insurance claim, keep track of all paperwork, medical bills, and correspondence relating to your claim in order to ensure you receive maximum disability benefits. Do not count on the government to keep track of your paperwork, things are lost, even electronically. The direction of your chain of command to keep your paperwork squared away, remains today. It's better than ever, but mistakes are made and nothing better helps veterans than having an organized set of the documents needed to pursue a claim.

Prior to March 24, 2015, the VA would accept "informal claims." These claims could be as simple as a handwritten note asking for benefits. For more information on claims submitted before March 24, 2015, head to "The New Process."

CLAIMS SUBMITTED BEFORE MARCH 24, 2015- OR THERE IS A HISTORY TO THIS!

On March 24th, 2015, the VA introduced a new system to standardize the VA benefits application process. This adjustment improved the time and efficiency of application decisions.

If you submitted a Formal claim before March 24, 2015, you must have submitted the following forms:

- VA Form 21-526, Veteran's Application for Compensation and/or Pension

- VA Form 21-526c, Pre-Discharge Compensation Claim

- VA Form 21-526EZ, Application for Disability Compensation and Related Compensation Benefits,

- VA Form 21-527EZ, Application for Pension

Before March 24, 2015, informal claims were extremely important to the claims process. Informal claims are only accepted if they were sent before March 24, 2015. There are many veterans who have pending claims that were established many years ago. My office has assisted many who have had claims in the system for over a decade! To be fair to the Veterans Administration, often times the older claims involved situations where paperwork was long lost, and who was to blame was and is a fair question. Moving paper files from one person to another is very time-consuming and if a file is separated from the rest of a claim file, it can take months or even years to locate and sometimes not at all. I attended a meeting in Washington, DC in 2009 where the Regional head of the VA was discussing the difficulty at that time of scanning all files, the agency was motivated but the funding wasn't sufficient to scan all files to allow more rapid processing. Instead, millions of dollars were spent shipping files from one place to another, sending them to copy centers when offices such as mine requested a copy of a Veterans C file. Not too long ago we received veterans claim files in boxes! Then it moved to CDs.

However, there have been many changes to the application process. It is important to note the VA may make changes in the process at any time, so you must stay up to date with the most current application process. Are you noticing a pattern?

So, why do you need to know about this? The informal claims process is no longer used, but it's always best practice to understand the historical interpretation of the law as you continue to work on your application.

INTENT TO FILE

Intent to File lets the VA know you are about to file a claim for benefits. It's an important date for many reasons. Firstly, once you submit an intent to file, you have one year to complete your claim before the VA closes it. Secondly, if you receive benefits, this is the date the VA legally decides you were due benefits and may receive back pay compensation. It is only required for Fully Developed Claim submissions.

An intent to file is a serious submission and should only be considered once you confirm you are eligible and prepared to submit a claim for benefits. There are three ways to submit an intent to file according to the Code of Federal Regulations.

- A saved electronic application
- Written VA Form 21-0966, or intent to file form
- Oral communication to a VA employee

When you submit an intent to file, we recommend using the online method. In fact, we recommend you use the online systems for the entire application process for organization and efficiency.

Importantly, an intent to file is unnecessary_for most benefit applications. Unless you have a clearly defined condition that unmistakably was caused by your service, an intent to file can often cause damage to your cases rather than help you. An example of an application where submitting an intent to file could increase your back paycheck is if you are missing a leg from an in-service injury.

APPLYING ONLINE

Before you begin, make sure you have gathered all your evidence for your claim. This will expedite your decision as well as prevent you from missing any deadlines.

Online application is easy! Here is how to apply for VA Disability Benefits online:

1) Log on to your VA account of your choice. *NOTE: Once you click the button to begin filling out your application, it will serve as your Intent to File letter. This leaves you one year from pushing this button to complete your application*

     i)   Login.gov

     ii)   ID.me

     iii)   DS Logon

     iv)   My HealtheVet

2) Fill out your VA Form 21-526EZ (Application for Disability Compensation and Related Compensation Benefits).

3) Submit your evidence and wait for communication from the VA about any further action needed for your application. Remember, the VA will only contact you if you do not fill out an FDC.

Of course, it gets complicated after your decision, and we will go in-depth about the decision appeal process late in the book.

APPLYING VIA MAIL

Although submitting your application online is preferred, the VA does still accept mail applications.

1) Submit your intent to file by completing one of the following

   a) Submitting a completed VA Form 21-0966, Intent to File a Claim for Compensation and/or Pension, or Survivors Pension and/or DIC. This form must be submitted in writing and signed by the Claimant as well as any Veterans

   Service Organization or VA-recognized Power of Attorney who helped you with your claim.

   b) Contacting a national call center(NCC)at 1-800-827-1000 or the National Pension Call Center (NPCC) at 1-877-294-6380

   c) Contacting a Veterans Service Center (VSC)/ Pension Management Center (PMC) employee by telephone or in-person.

2) Complete the paper application of the Application for Disability Compensation and Related Compensation Benefits, or VA Form 21-526EZ.

3) Submit the application through one of the following ways

    a)   Mail the application to
            U.S. Department of Veterans Affairs
            Claims Intake Center
            PO Box 4444
            Janesville, WI 53547-4444

    b)   Fax it to
            (844) 531-7818 (inside the U.S.)
            (248) 524-4260 (outside the U.S.)

    c)   Turn it in in-person at your local
            regional office.

4) Your application is submitted! Again, you then can wait for communication from the VA regarding anything else needed to prove your claim.

Here is the summary;

Here are some tips for better-receiving benefits based on the information in the text:

1. Stay informed: The VA benefits application process can change at any time, so it's important to stay up to date on the most current application process. Make sure to research and read up on the most recent requirements and forms needed to file a claim.

2. Keep organized: It's crucial to keep track of all paperwork, medical bills, and correspondence relating to your claim. This will help you to ensure that you receive maximum disability benefits. Make sure to keep a record of

all important documents and to file them in an organized way.

3. Submit a formal claim: As of March 24th, 2015, you must submit a formal claim for your benefits by submitting the Veteran's Application for Disability, Compensation, and Related Compensation benefits (VA Form 21-526EZ). Be sure to include all necessary documentation such as marriage certificates, birth certificates, and doctor's reports when submitting your application.

4. Consider using an online application: Applying for benefits online can be a more efficient and organized process. You can use various online systems such as login.gov, ID.me, DS Logon, or My HealtheVet to apply for benefits. Be sure to gather all the necessary evidence for your claim before starting your online application.

5. Submit an Intent to File if necessary: An Intent to File is only required for Fully Developed Claim submissions. Make sure to confirm your eligibility and preparedness to submit a claim for benefits before submitting an Intent to File.

6. Seek assistance: If you're having difficulty understanding or completing the application process, seek assistance from a Veterans Service Organization or VA-recognized Power of Attorney. They can help you navigate the application process and ensure that you submit a complete and accurate claim.

By following these tips, you can increase your chances of successfully receiving benefits for yourself and your family members.

WHY ONLINE IS BETTER

The online application process is recommended for veterans. It has useful online programs to track your claim, view prescription records, and submit evidence to help organize your claim.

A more organized claim is reviewed quicker, getting you your claim decision sooner.

If you prefer, you can also submit your VA Form 21-526EZ in person or via mail. To find a VA Administration office near you, You can locate your nearest office by visiting va.gov/directory. Alternatively, you can mail your application via mail to the address below.

Department of Veterans Affairs
Claims Intake Center
PO Box 4444
Janesville, WI 53547-4444

ADDITIONAL FORMS

Your initial application is just the easy part. The VA Form 21-526EZ is just the first step in applying for benefits. You may need additional forms depending on the type of claim you file. Review your claim carefully to submit all the forms you need correctly in your first application. This will get your claim reviewed quicker and help you get the benefits you need.

Claiming PTSD
- VA Form 21-0781

Claiming Additional Benefits for Your Spouse
- VA Form 21-2680

Claiming Dependents
- VA Form 21-686c

If your child is in school and between the ages of 18-23
Authorizing the Release of your Medical Records
- VA Form 21-4142

You also need to include evidence with your application. Some examples of VA evidence to include are
- VA records (state and federal)

- Medical treatment records

- Supporting statements

  - These are statements from family members, friends, and community members who can confirm your disability or illness.

This evidence can be uploaded online using the QuickSubmit tool with your Access VA account.

ONLINE RESOURCES

The VA office is notoriously slow. When it comes to something as vital as a disability claim, knowing the instant your claim has been reviewed is vital to getting the assistance you need.

What are the online resources for veterans to pursue disability benefits?

There are several online resources that veterans can use to pursue disability benefits:

1. Department of Veterans Affairs (VA) website: The VA website provides information on eligibility requirements

and the disability benefits process. Veterans can also file claims and track the status of their claims on the website.

2. Veterans Benefits Administration (VBA): The VBA provides information and assistance to veterans on a variety of benefits, including disability benefits.

3. eBenefits: eBenefits is an online portal for veterans to access their VA benefits and information. It allows veterans to apply for benefits, track the status of their claims, and access their VA letters and other important documents.

4. VA Regional Offices: VA Regional Offices provide local assistance to veterans in their area and can assist with the disability benefits process.

5. Veterans Service Organizations (VSOs): VSOs are organizations that assist veterans in navigating the VA benefits process, including disability benefits. Some VSOs have online resources and tools to help veterans with their claims.

6. Lawyers who specialize in veterans law: Lawyers who specialize in veterans law can provide legal representation and assistance to veterans in the disability benefits process.

By using these online resources, veterans can access information and assistance to help them pursue disability benefits. It is important to note that some of these resources may have limitations based on a veteran's specific circumstances and that it is recommended to consult with a qualified professional to ensure the best outcome.

The VA Claim Tracker isn't just free–it's also easy to use!

1) Go to your "My VA" Dashboard on the top right corner of the page once you've signed in to any of the above accounts

2) Scroll down the page to the "Track Claims" section to view the status of any open claims or appeals you have.

3) Click on "View Status" to view supporting evidence and a more detailed status update on your claim. Here you can view

    a) Doctor visits

    b) Prescriptions

    c) File appeals

These online tools are also helpful in scheduling and canceling appointments:

- Request approved community care
- View future and print a list of your future appointments
- Find the VA or community care facility for your appointments

Overall, it's best to make these accounts before you even apply for benefits. I understand how confusing technology can be sometimes. However, I cannot stress enough how much easier this process is if you choose to use the online application system.

I explain more on this earlier in "Why Online is Better."

THE VA'S DUTY TO NOTIFY AND ASSIST

What is the VA's Duty to Notify and Assist and how can it help my case?

The VA's Duty to Notify and Assist is a legal obligation that requires the Department of Veterans Affairs (VA) to provide veterans with information and assistance throughout the disability benefits process.

This duty includes:

1. Providing information: The VA must provide veterans with information about their rights and the disability benefits process, including information about the types of evidence that will be considered in their claim.

2. Assisting with the claim: The VA must assist veterans in obtaining the evidence needed to support their claims, such as medical records and statements from witnesses. The VA is also required to advise veterans about what evidence is necessary to support their claim and to assist in obtaining that evidence.

3. Notifying veterans of decisions: The VA must provide veterans with written notice of the decision on their claim and the reasons for that decision.

By fulfilling its Duty to Notify and Assist, the VA is helping to ensure that veterans are informed and have the necessary information to pursue their disability benefits claim. This can help veterans to better understand the process and the evidence required to support their claim, which can improve their chances of success in the disability benefits process.

It is important to note that while the VA has a legal obligation to fulfill its Duty to Notify and Assist, veterans may still need to take an active role in pursuing their disability benefits claim and obtaining the evidence necessary to support their claim. An attorney who specializes in veterans law can assist veterans in navigating the disability benefits process and fulfilling the VA's Duty to Notify and Assist.

The VA won't leave this entirely up to you. Thanks to the Veterans Claims and Assistance Act of 2000, the VA does have a duty to notify and assist you on your claim, but only to a certain extent.

Most importantly, the VA will only help you if your application is "substantially complete." According to 38 CFR 3.159(a)(3) of the Veterans Claims and Assistance Act, this is defined as an application including your name, sufficient service information, at least one named medical condition, and your signature. If your application is not "substantially complete," the VA does have a duty to notify you of missing information required to finish your application.

The VA won't just notify you of anything that might be helpful for your case. It will only do the bare minimum.

Overall, this is a nice gesture, but DON'T rely on the VA to notify and assist you. It is in your best interest to stay on top of your case yourself.

EVIDENCE

What is the evidence that needs to be submitted in a VA claim and how do you get that evidence?

The evidence that needs to be submitted in a VA claim depends on the specific circumstances of the claim and the condition for which the veteran is seeking benefits. Some of the types of evidence that may be required in a VA claim include:

1. Medical records: Medical records from private providers, the VA, or military service are required to support a claim for disability benefits. These records should include a diagnosis of the condition, the severity of the condition, and any treatments received.

2. Lay evidence: Lay evidence includes statements from friends, family members, and other individuals who can provide information about the veteran's condition and how it affects their daily life.

3. Service medical records: Service medical records, such as the veteran's service treatment records and service personnel records, are required to establish a link between the veteran's current condition and their military service.

4. Medical opinions: Medical opinions from private providers or the VA may be required to support the veteran's claim. These opinions should provide information about the severity of the veteran's condition and how it affects their ability to work.

To obtain this evidence, veterans can start by contacting their private healthcare providers and requesting copies of their medical records. If the veteran received treatment through the VA, they can request their VA medical records through the VA's Health Information Management Service. Service medical records can be obtained through the National Personnel Records Center.

It is important to note that the VA may also require additional evidence depending on the specific circumstances of the claim. An attorney who specializes in veterans' law can assist veterans in obtaining the necessary evidence to support their claim and maximizing their chances of success in the VA disability benefits process.

Submitting evidence is absolutely essential to building a successful VA case. However, the VA has very specific guidelines for evidence as well as a particular system for weighing evidence that can feel counterintuitive or overwhelming to applicants.

First, we must define evidence. According to the Merriam-Webster dictionary, it is defined as "A sign which shows that something exists or is true." In the VA, the evidence you submit should support the claim that an event or circumstance

- Happened at a certain time,
- Occurred in a certain place, and
- Involved a certain individual.

Think about it like this: Your disability claim should prove your condition or illness was caused - either directly or indirectly– by your service **and** that it now requires treatment and support which you cannot provide. You must prove both statements with strong, relevant evidence to receive the compensation you need.

Overall, the evidence for your claim must support a "Clear and Unmistakable" connection according to the Code of Federal Regulations. Legally, this is defined as evidence that reasonable minds conclude supports your claim. This concept is particularly useful if your records were somehow destroyed or if your condition wasn't reported during service;

for example, a reasonable mind could conclude that if your medical records demonstrate the symptoms of a condition, you likely had it even if no doctor diagnosed or reported you with it.

Once the VA receives your evidence, it will weigh (or consider) it in a particular way based on its ability to prove a fact. The evidence is first sorted into two categories: primary evidence and secondary evidence.

PRIMARY EVIDENCE

Primary evidence is the most valuable and high-ranked evidence you can provide for your case and encompasses first-hand documentation such as in-service medical records and service personnel records (which could show time the client had to miss due to injury.) Primary evidence is crucial to VA cases and should be provided whenever available.

Examples of primary evidence include

- Daily Staff Journals
- Monthly Summary and Reports
- Information from VBA-sanctioned websites
- Even medals/rewards earned in-service

These are just a few examples of primary evidence that you should include in your claim. Again, the goal of this evidence is to establish that it is "at least as likely as not," that your injury or illness was caused by your service. This is called the "nexus" of your claim and, without it, your claim *will* be denied.

SECONDARY EVIDENCE

You may not have primary evidence available –and that's not the end of the world. The VA will also accept secondary evidence for your claim! The VA understands military medical records can be incomplete, in these cases, secondary evidence can help support your claim.

Secondary evidence is evidence by someone who has not observed the fact, but can attest to its effects or corroborate that it happened. There are two pieces of secondary evidence to include in your VA claim:

- Lay Evidence (like buddy letters!)
- Medical Evidence

For secondary evidence to be considered, it must be "competent."

According to the Code of Federal Regulations, Competent medical evidence is defined as:

"... evidence provided by a person who is qualified through education, training, or experience to offer medical diagnoses, statements, or opinions. Competent medical evidence may also mean statements conveying sound medical principles found in medical treatises. It would also include statements contained in authoritative writings such as medical and scientific articles and research reports or analyses."

In other words, competent medical evidence is lay secondary evidence from a qualified medical professional. According to the Federal Code of Regulations, Competent Lay evidence is defined as:

> "...evidence not requiring that the proponent have specialized education, training, or experience. Lay evidence is competent if it is provided by a person who has knowledge of facts or circumstances and conveys matters that can be observed and described by a lay person."

This is the same as competent medical evidence, but the author does not need to have medical expertise.

Although primary evidence is preferred, secondary evidence can help your case in situations where primary evidence is absent or destroyed. Military medical records can be spotty or incomplete. On the battlefield, the upkeep of medical records simply does not take top priority. In these cases, the VA will accept secondary evidence. Occasionally, your records can get lost or destroyed in a fire. For example, in 1973, a large fire destroyed the records of thousands of Army and Air Force veterans at the National Personnel Records Center (NPRC) in St. Louis Missouri. Sometimes injuries and illnesses don't get documented in the first place.

LAY EVIDENCE

Lay evidence is evidence from a non-qualified individual or organization that supports your claim. It is not heavily weighted (or considered) by the VA because of the lack of expertise of the person providing it. However, there are special considerations for Lay evidence in cases. Just like secondary evidence, Lay evidence can become vital for your claim if your records were destroyed or lost at some point after you were discharged.

Originally, Lay Evidence was considered very weak evidence in a veteran's claim. Claim reviewers would consider the evidence irrelevant and focus on the medical evidence provided. However, recent legal cases as well as the Veterans Claims Assistance Act of 2000 changed this process. While Lay Evidence is still not as highly weighted as Primary Evidence, it is now accepted as valid evidence, especially in cases where primary evidence is lacking.

Here are some tips and summary;

Tips to better receive benefits as a veteran:

1. Use the online application process: This process has useful online programs that can help you track your claim, view prescription records, and submit evidence to help organize your claim. A more organized claim is reviewed quicker, which can get you your claim decision sooner.

2. Submit all necessary forms with your initial application: The VA Form 21-526EZ is just the first step in applying for benefits. You may need additional forms depending on the type of claim you file. Review your claim carefully to submit all the forms you need correctly in your first application. This will get your claim reviewed quicker and help you get the benefits you need.

3. Use online resources: There are several online resources that veterans can use to pursue disability benefits, such as the VA website, eBenefits, VA Regional Offices, and Veterans Service Organizations (VSOs). Lawyers who specialize in veterans law can also provide legal

representation and assistance to veterans in the disability benefits process.

4. Stay on top of your case: Although the VA has a duty to notify and assist you, it is in your best interest to stay on top of your case yourself. This includes submitting all necessary forms and evidence, regularly checking the status of your claim, and contacting the VA or a qualified professional for assistance when needed.

5. Submit strong and relevant evidence: The evidence you submit should support the claim that an event or circumstance happened at a certain time, occurred in a certain place, and involved a certain individual. The evidence for your claim must support a "Clear and Unmistakable" connection according to the Code of Federal Regulations. This means that reasonable minds must conclude that your evidence supports your claim. Submitting primary evidence is preferred, but secondary evidence and lay evidence can also help support your claim in situations where primary evidence is absent or incomplete.

There are four main kinds of lay evidence to consider submitting:

- Buddy Letters
- Spouse and Coworker Letters
- Personal Statements

Below, find explanations and guides on how to write your own lay evidence statements for your claim.

BUDDY LETTER

The buddy letter is the main avenue for submitting secondary evidence. Presented in VA Form 21-4138, the buddy letter is a fairly open-ended statement where a witness to your service- related issues can describe both the details of the event and the way it has impacted your life as a result.

A good buddy letter should do several things:

1. Establish a clear relationship between the claimant and the person writing on their behalf.

2. Describe the incident in detail–what is the who, what, why, where, when, and how? What was done in terms of treatment?

3. Clearly state how the incident has affected you. Compare and contrast life before and after: how has it affected your ability to work, quality of life, and so on?

Importantly, a buddy letter can not confirm any medical facts. For example, your buddy can't write that your exposure to loud planes caused hearing loss which contributes to your migraines. Instead, they can just attest to the intense noise you were exposed to while in service.

SPOUSE AND COWORKER STATEMENTS

Like buddy letters, a Spouse and/or Coworker Statement is submitted with VA Form 21-4138. These statements can corroborate your daily symptoms or a change in life activities or personality after service. However, just like the Buddy Letter, these statements cannot confirm medical facts. Focus on details, especially numerical ones. For example, if you struggle with migraines and frequently need to rest, your spouse could attest that you often sleep for three to four hours to recover from your migraines.

PERSONAL STATEMENTS

Personal statements again are submitted with VA Form 21-4138. These statements are 3-5 paragraphs long that detail the narrative of your service and your present conditions. In your statement, you should include.

- The disabilities you are claiming

- Your time frame of service

- Your experiences and duties in service relevant to your disabilities

- The time frame of your disabilities

- Your current symptoms from your disabilities

- The impact of your symptoms and disabilities

Again, in this statement, you can not confirm medical evidence. You can only explain or elaborate on *your* experiences. For example, rather than stating that you have hearing loss caused by your service, elaborate on the hours you worked around planes and were exposed to loud noises. Then, explain when you first experienced *symptoms* of hearing loss.

While it's not required, we also recommend including any awards or medals you received while in service. <u>These details corroborate your service dates as well as establish your good character</u> for the VA Claim reviewer.

These may seem like small details, but these are the things the VA looks for when determining if the evidence for your claim is competent.

MEDICAL NEXUS OR MEDICAL EVIDENCE

We will go into more detail on Medical Nexus letters further on in the book, but these are letters from a qualified professional proving that it is "at least as likely as not" your condition was caused or worsened by your time in service.

As you will read in the next section, statements from a qualified medical professional are vital to proving your claim with secondary evidence. Without these medical statements, it will be impossible to prove your claim.

CHAPTER SIX

WORKING WITH DOCTORS FOR YOUR APPLICATION

C&P EXAMS

A Compensation and Pension exam (or C&P exam) is a medical examination of a veteran performed by the VA. If you are asked to complete one for your application DO IT. It will be used against you in your claim if you refuse one.

During the examination, the VA examiner will complete a Disability and Benefits Questionnaire or DBQ. Before your exam, you should look up your disabilities in the code of federal regulations and the DBQ to know what is required to prove your condition.

On the next page is an example of a DBQ for heart conditions.

SECTION I - DIAGNOSIS

Note: These are condition(s) for which an evaluation has been requested on the exam request form (Internal VA) or for which the Veteran has requested medical evidence be provided for submission to VA.

1A. List the claimed conditions that pertain to this questionnaire:

Note: These are the diagnoses determined during this current evaluation of the claimed condition(s) listed above. If there is no diagnosis, if the diagnosis is different from a previous diagnosis for this condition, or if there is a diagnosis of a complication due to the claimed condition, explain your findings and reasons in the remarks section. Date of diagnosis can be the date of the evaluation if the clinician is making the initial diagnosis or an approximate date determined through record review or reported history.

1B. Select diagnoses associated with the claimed condition(s) (check all that apply):

☐ The Veteran does not have a current diagnosis associated with any claimed conditions listed above. (Explain your findings and reasons in the remarks section)

		ICD Code:	Date of diagnosis:
☐	Acute, subacute, or old myocardial infarction		
☐	Atherosclerotic cardiovascular disease		
☐	Unstable angina		
☐	Stable angina		
☐	Arteriosclerotic heart disease (Coronary artery disease)		
☐	Coronary spasm, including Prinzmetal's angina		
☐	Congestive heart failure		
☐	Bradycardia (bradyarrhythmia)		
☐	Ventricular arrhythmia		
☐	Supraventricular arrhythmia (supraventricular tachycardia)		
☐	Automatic implantable cardioverter defibrillator (AICD)		
☐	Implanted cardiac pacemaker		
☐	Cardiac/Heart transplant		
☐	Valvular heart disease		
☐	Heart block		
☐	Other infectious heart conditions		
☐	Hyperthyroid heart disease (if checked also complete the Thyroid/Parathyroid questionnaire)		
☐	Syphilitic heart disease		
☐	Pericarditis		
☐	Endocarditis		
☐	Rheumatic heart disease		
☐	Active valvular infection		
☐	Coronary artery bypass graft		
☐	Heart valve replacement (prosthesis)		
☐	Cardiomyopathy		
☐	Hypertensive heart disease		
☐	Pericardial adhesions		
☐	Other heart condition (specify)		
	Other diagnosis #1		
	Other diagnosis #2		
	Other diagnosis #3		

If there are additional diagnoses that pertain to heart conditions, list using above format:

SECTION II - MEDICAL HISTORY

2A. Describe the history (including onset and course) of the Veteran's heart condition (brief summary):

2B. Do any of the Veteran's heart conditions qualify within the generally accepted medical definition of Ischemic Heart Disease (IHD)? ☐ Yes ☐ No

DISABILITY BENEFITS QUESTIONNAIRES (OR DBQS)

Disability Benefits Questionnaires (DBQs) are public forms outlining questions that the VA health professionals or your doctor should answer during a C&P exam. I explained this in the previous section, but they are also useful for much more!

These forms are almost a cheat sheet to help you understand what the VA is looking for to prove your claim. It's *always* in your best interest to look up the DBQ for your disabilities.

You can easily access the DBQ for any condition through the Code of Federal Regulations. Again, an example of a DBQ for heart conditions is available above.

NEXUS LETTERS

What should be in a Nexus letter to support a VA disability claim?

A nexus letter is a medical opinion that is used to support a VA disability claim. It should be written by a qualified healthcare provider who has treated or examined the veteran. A well- written nexus letter should include the following information:

1. The veteran's medical history: The healthcare provider should describe the veteran's medical history, including any prior treatments, diagnoses, and surgeries.

2. A diagnosis of the condition: The healthcare provider should provide a current diagnosis of the veteran's condition, including any relevant diagnostic tests or examinations.

3. A link between the condition and military service: The healthcare provider should provide a clear and convincing explanation of how the veteran's condition relates to their military service, if applicable.

4. The severity of the condition: The healthcare provider should describe the severity of the veteran's condition, including any symptoms and how they affect the veteran's daily life and ability to work.

5. The impact of the condition on the veteran's ability to work: The healthcare provider should provide an opinion on the veteran's ability to work and perform daily activities, including any limitations they may have.

It is important to note that a nexus letter should be written in a clear and concise manner and should be supported by the veteran's medical records and other relevant evidence. An attorney who specializes in veterans law can assist veterans in obtaining a well-written nexus letter that will support their VA disability claim.

Nexus letters are letters from your doctor that link your condition to your service.

WHAT IS A NEXUS LETTER?

According to the VA, the definition of "nexus" is "link." Therefore, a nexus letter links your condition back to your service. A nexus letter is a letter from a professional corroborating your condition to the VA to increase your chance of receiving benefits. These letters can make or break your claim for benefits and it's vital to get one when you can. If you are submitting a claim for a secondary condition, a medical nexus letter is required to link how this secondary condition was caused by your service.

WHO AND HOW TO ASK

Firstly, it's important to ask the right people for a nexus letter. If you are claiming benefits for PTSD or Anxiety, a nexus letter from a general practitioner may not do you any good. Look for a professional. For example, if you have a heart condition, ask a cardiologist for a nexus letter, and so on. This means your family doctor may not be able to provide the kind of nexus letter you need to truly help your claim.

Next, how to ask for a nexus letter. Asking a doctor for a nexus letter can seem daunting. If the doctor is affiliated with the VA, they should have the experience to write you a nexus letter or direct you to a physician who can. If they are a private practice, they may be less willing.

Currently, there is no database of doctors who are willing to write a nexus letter for veterans. If your doctor refuses to write a nexus letter, ask other veteran friends which physicians they would recommend. However, the more work you do, the more likely they are to write one out. Here are some tips to ask for a nexus letter from your doctor.

1. Research a qualified doctor. This means someone who is going to have the knowledge and medical research to provide the best evidence for your case. (Don't be afraid to ask friends for recommendations!)

2. Outline exactly what needs to be in the nexus letter. Often, non-VA doctors can be intimidated by the idea of writing a nexus letter. By clearly outlining what needs to be included, or even writing one yourself, you can improve your chances of receiving a letter for your claim.

    a. The physician's credentials that outline they are a reliable source for this information.

    b. A reference to your medical records to indicate they have reviewed them.

    c. The doctor's opinion.

    d. The medical rationale supports the doctor's opinion.

NEXUS LETTER

On the next page, is an example of a successful Nexus letter. You can go online as well to find templates that you can give your doctor to help ensure your letter helps your case. You can easily find more examples and tips to write the most effective nexus letter possible. Remember, research is key to creating an effective claim!

Date 06/06/2022

To Whom it may concern,

I am [REDACTED] I am board certified in my specialty since 1985.
My credentials are included. I have been asked to write a statement in support of the aforementioned Veteran's disability claim.

I have personally reviewed records and have medical history (X-rays and history of occurrence). I have also reviewed and noted the circumstances and events of his military service in the time period February 2015 - February 2016 to determine if there is a direct correlation for his disability claim resulting from carrying heavy back packs and wearing military boots, without support, while he served during his military service.

[REDACTED] is a patient under my care and has been since 12/06/2018. Not only has his conditions resulted in severe pain, it also has manifested into chronic bursitis, degenerative hip joints , osteophytic knees, avulsion fracture left knee (Osgood Schlatter), stress fracture L5 pars and altered gait, which in turns effects the entire musculoskeletal system due to imbalance.
I am familiar with his history and have examined [REDACTED] on different occasions while he has been under my care.

[REDACTED] has no other known risk factors or know occurrences that may have precipitated his current condition.

After a review of the pertinent records it is of my personal opinion that it is more likely as not that Mr. [REDACTED] condition is a direct result of his carrying excessive weight in a back pack and wearing military boots during his military service.

There are no other records available or known of that suggest any other incident that would have created his current conditions that are under examination for his disability claim.

If needed, you can contact me personally at my office for any further information.

MAKING AN APPOINTMENT WITH THE VA DOCTORS

Need to see a specialist? The VA appointments tool can help you schedule an appointment as well as:

- Schedule and cancel pre-approved non-VA appointments

- Request approved community care

- View and print a list of your future appointments

- Find the VA community care facility for your appointments

Not all appointments can be made online, but this tool can help you visit the doctors you need sooner, getting you the care and treatment you need.

To use this tool,

1. Go to your "My VA" Dashboard on the top right corner of the page once you've signed in to any of the above accounts

2. From here, you can schedule and view appointments from your MyVA

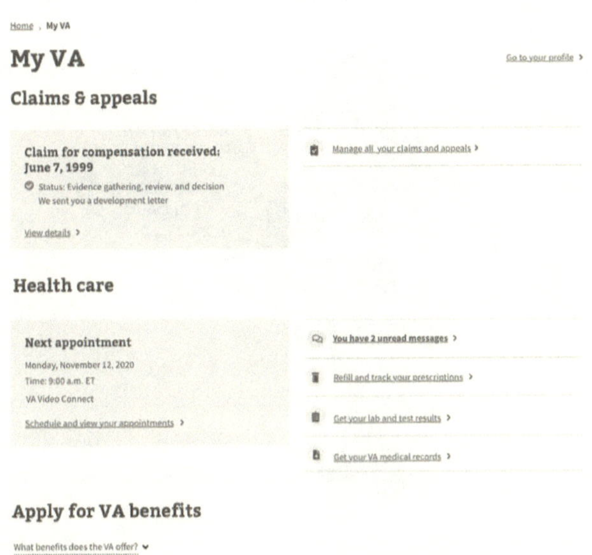

DON'T UNDERESTIMATE THE EVIDENCE

Do not expect the VA to have all the evidence required for your case in your medical records. In some instances like a missing limb from an in-service injury, that may be enough. However, in most cases, you must seek out other forms of evidence to prove your case.

Evidence isn't something that you can just expect the VA to have on your file. For the best results, you must seek out the most effective methods to receive what is required to prove your claim and get the benefits you need.

By reading this book, you are taking the first steps in finding out what those methods are.

For more complicated claims or if you are seeking a high rating for a non-presumptive condition, it's recommended you seek a lawyer to help with this process. Evidence is what proves the facts of your case, and not submitting certain pieces or submitting them late can make or break your application.

CHAPTER SEVEN

HOW THE VA RATES YOUR APPLICATION

After you have submitted your application for veteran benefits, the VA will rate each claim based on two things:

1. If the injury or condition is service-connected, and

2. The severity of the injury or condition.

If the VA decides your injury or condition is service-connected, you will receive a "Rating Decision" between 10 percent and 100 percent. The percentage awarded is based on the schedules contained in the "38 CFR Book C Schedule for Rating Decisions." You can view this book at <u>benefits.va.gov/warms/bookc.asp</u>

The VA Rating Schedule is divided into categories based on the system within the body and then broken down into subcategories. Under each subcategory is a list of symptoms or disabilities associated with this subsection. These symptoms and disabilities are categorized by what percentage the VA will reward.

The below graphic is a snippet from the Rating Schedule for diseases of the ear. The number on the right side indicates the Rating Percentage for that disease.

DISEASES OF THE EAR

Rating

6200 Chronic suppurative otitis media, mastoiditis, or cholesteatoma
(or any combination):

  During suppuration, or with aural polyps — 10

  Note: Evaluate hearing impairment, and complications such as labyrinthitis, tinnitus, facial nerve paralysis, or bone loss of skull, separately.

6201 Chronic nonsuppurative otitis media with effusion (serous otitis media):

  Rate hearing impairment

6202 Otosclerosis:

  Rate hearing impairment

6204 Peripheral vestibular disorders:

  Dizziness and occasional staggering — 30
  Occasional dizziness — 10

  Note: Objective findings supporting the diagnosis of vestibular disequilibrium are required before a compensable evaluation can be assigned under this code. Hearing impairment or suppuration shall be separately rated and combined.

6205 Meniere's syndrome (endolymphatic hydrops):

  Hearing impairment with attacks of vertigo and cerebellar gait occurring more than once weekly, with or without tinnitus — 100
  Hearing impairment with attacks of vertigo and cerebellar gait occurring from one to four times a month, with or without tinnitus — 60
  Hearing impairment with vertigo less than once a month, with or without tinnitus — 30

  Note: Evaluate Meniere's syndrome either under these criteria or by separately evaluating vertigo (as a peripheral vestibular disorder), hearing impairment, and tinnitus, whichever method results in a higher overall evaluation. But do not combine an evaluation for hearing impairment, tinnitus, or vertigo with an evaluation under diagnostic code 6205.

CHAPTER EIGHT

COMBINING VETERANS DISABILITY WITH SOCIAL SECURITY DISABILITY

The Department of Veterans Affairs and Social Security Office both have programs to help receive benefits based on injuries or illnesses you have. Receiving benefits from the VA does not necessarily exclude you from the benefits that Social Security offers for wounded veterans. Both programs can offer the support and care you need to live your life.

Social Security Disability (SSD) and VA Disability both require you to prove specific aspects of your disability. What they require to prove your disability differs because the goal of each program is not the same. Therefore, while the VA requires you to prove your disability is connected to your service, the Social Security Administration (SSA) requires you to prove your illness or disability prevents you from having "Substantial Gainful Employment." For this reason, if Social Security finds you "disabled," and the medical reasons for this decision are all service-connected, the VA cannot disregard the Social Security decision. Since Social Security claims typically resolve faster than VA claims, this may help

you with your VA claim. A rating from VA can also improve your evidence for an SSD claim.

The programs also work collaboratively to help you receive the support you need. For example, if you've sent medical records to the VA, they will send them over to SSA once you begin a disability claim with the SSA. SSA also provides priority processing if you are a Wounded Warrior or Military Casualty, as well as if you have a 100% disability rating with the VA.

It is important to note that both programs have different definitions of disability; so, qualifying for one program does not make you automatically eligible for another. For example, receiving VA benefits because your disability is service-connected may not qualify you for Social Security disability if it does not inhibit your ability to maintain "gainful employment." The good news is that your decision on either claim will not affect the benefits from another program. For example, receiving an increased VA rating will not decrease your SSDI benefits. Having a VA rating also improves your chances of receiving SSDI benefits. Total Disability Individual Unemployability (TDIU).

WHAT IS TDIU?

A veteran may file for TDIU when he or she is not working and unable to work because of a service-connected condition or injury. TDIU can provide you with Health Care benefits as well as payments to help support you.

To qualify for TDIU you must:

- Already have one service-connect disability rated 60% or higher OR have multiple service-connected disabilities with one or more rated 40% or higher with a total rating of 70%

- And you must prove you are unable to maintain substantially gainful employment because of the disability.

Occasionally, you may qualify for TDIU with a lower disability rating if you need to frequently stay in a hospital because of your illness or disability.

A veteran may apply for TDIU online through eBenefits or at their local VA office. Or, call me, my team is happy to help!

APPLYING FOR TDIU

There are two forms to fill out for TDIU. First is the Veteran's Application for Increased Compensation Based on Unemployability, or VA Form 21-8940. This four-page form can be found on the VA website and requires you to tell the VA of your previous employers and loss of payment due to illness for each previous job as well as explain the details of your illness. It is vital to explain your position as specifically as possible, calling previous employers when applicable to get the information you need.

You also need to complete a Request for Employment Information in Connection with Claim for Disability Benefits, or VA Form 21-4192. This is a two-page document for all employers you listed on VA Form 21-8940 to fill out. Don't worry if your employer doesn't send this form back! While it is beneficial to your claim, the VA cannot deny your TDIU claim because an employer did not send back a form.

You may also benefit by submitting VA Form 21-4138. This form is only for friends, family members, or former service members who served alongside the veteran and can attest to your disability and inability to work. For example, if you have a spouse, they could provide a statement explaining how they see your disability hindering your ability to work.

Just like other VA benefits applications, you can submit a TDIU application online or in person. As outlined in the sections "applying online" and "Applying Via Mail."

If the veteran chooses to apply via eBenefits, he or she must print a Form 21-4192 for their previous employer to complete. Send the completed form to the VA. The VA is required to consider TDIU if the veteran is not working and has at least one condition at 60% or has a combination of 70%, which includes one condition rated at 40% or higher.

AN INTRODUCTION TO SOCIAL SECURITY DISABILITY

Since many veterans have disabilities that are having a substantial impact on working, understanding the social security disability process is important and should be considered anytime a VA claim is made. Remember, as discussed before, the systems share some similarities but are in operation different. With Veterans' Disability claims and unemployability, you must demonstrate a service connection. With Social Security, those connections are irrelevant.

A STARTING POINT

After a diagnosis of an illness or an accident involving an injury, you may find yourself worrying about how you will pay your bills. For some situations, receiving benefits from Social Security or private disability may be the solution. For many of our clients, the ability to obtain disability benefits is crucial in order to <u>provide basics in life</u>, such as food, shelter, clothing, and medical care. These benefits also provide the ability to enjoy certain freedoms in life such as special occasions, gifts, and even vacations. In many cases, time is of the essence and it is important that those who suffer from a disability understand the systems they are dealing with so they can adequately protect their family.

CHAPTER NINE

WHAT IS SOCIAL SECURITY DISABILITY?

Social Security Disability is a payroll tax-funded, federal insurance program of the United States government. When an individual is unable to work due to an impairment that individual may qualify for Social Security Disability (SSD). However, there are two types of Social Security Disability: a) Social Security Disability Insurance (SSDI also known as DIB) and Supplemental Security Income (SSI also known as DI).

A. Types of Social Security Disability Benefits

    1.   Social Security Disability Insurance (also known as DIB)

        a.   SSDI provides disability benefits to individuals who have earned enough work credits to qualify. As such, a claimant's past fifteen years of work history is relevant but when a person last worked is most important. SSDI only ensures benefits to a claimant for four years after they have stopped working. This means for a person to qualify for SSDI they must be found disabled prior to the expiration of four years after they stopped working. Once they qualify within that period the claimant will be eligible for SSDI payments until they are no longer disabled.

b. The amount of money a claimant receives from SSDI on a monthly basis varies for each individual. The amount is determined by a formula based on how much a claimant has paid into Social Security taxes. This means if a person worked but did not pay any social security taxes they will not be eligible for SSDI payments. The maximum benefit a claimant may receive in 2023 is $3,627.00.

2. DI (SSI)

a. SSI was created for low-income individuals who either have not worked, have not earned sufficient work credits, or have become disabled after their SSDI insurance period has run.

b. Unlike SSDI, in addition to being found disabled medically, to qualify for SSI a claimant must also meet financial requirements. For an individual they must not have a household income of more than $733 a month and for a married claimant may not have a household income of more than $1100.

1. Household income can include assistance by household members or others such as food and shelter, ownership of

an additional home beside a homestead, ownership of a car beside one personal vehicle, money in a checking or savings account, stocks and bonds, VA benefits received, Workers' Compensation benefits received, a spouse's income, ownership in items worth more than $2,000 for individuals (excluding exceptions above) and $3,000 for couples (excluding exceptions above).

   c. The amount of money a claimant receives from SSI on a monthly basis is set statewide. Though an individual may receive a different amount based upon specific details of their financial situation. Currently, in 2015, the most a claimant may receive monthly under SSI 2015 is $733.00 for an individual and $1100.00 for a couple.

3.   Medicare

   a. An claimant who qualifies for SSDI will receive Medicare two years after the date they started to receive or two after the date they should have started to receive SSDI benefits.

4.   Medicaid

   a. A claimant who qualifies for SSI will receive Medicaid benefits immediately. However, a claimant must contact their local Department of Children and Families for what to do to ensure Medicaid benefits.

Social Security Administration will only pay for disabilities that are "total" disabilities and will not pay for a disability that is partial or short-term.

"Disability" under Social Security usually requires that:

- You cannot do the work that you did before;

- You cannot adjust to other work because of your conditions; and

- Your disability has lasted or is expected to last for at least one year, or result in death

There are some medical situations where even if you are able to work you may still qualify for Social Security. It's referred to as meeting or exceeding a listing under the Social Security regulations.

WHERE DOES DISABILITY BEGIN?

The definition of disability varies depending on the system. For instance, Social Security Administration may have a different definition than a private disability policy. Generally, in any system of disability, the person seeking compensation must be unable to work. There are some very narrow situations that may allow for a small amount of work. However, practically speaking, if you are working then you will not qualify for any disability program that rests on an inability to work. This seems like a simple concept, but to many, it can cause a tangle of confusion.

A. How is a Person Disabled?

    1. General 5-step process

a. Has not engaged in SGA (Substantial Gain-
    ful Employment)

    1. The claimant must not have earned more
        than $1130 in a month. Typically this is
        satisfied by the claimant no longer work-
        ing. However, if a claimant works 4 hours
        a week due to their condition making $9
        dollars an hour, they likely will not make
        SGA.

b. Impairment severe

    1. The conditions must last at least 12
        months. If a claimant's condition gets
        better after 9 months they will not be
        eligible for disability.

c. Impairment meets or equals listing

    1. SSA has a list of conditions that if a
        claimant has certain medically docu-
        mented symptoms, SSA will find the
        claimant automatically disabled.

        a. Medically documented doesn't mean
            the claimant's complaints per se but
            what a doctor through examination,
            testing, and/or evaluation finds the
            claimant's symptoms to be.

    2. Click https://www.ssa.gov/disability/
        professionals/bluebook/AdultListings.
        htm for a list of the listings and the
        symptoms a claimant must have.

3. When signing a case it is always important to consider the claimant's symptoms and if the symptoms are medically documented.

d. RFC to perform past relevant work

1. Residual Functional Capacity is the most you can do despite your conditions and limitations. At this step. the adjudicator determines if you can return to past relevant work.

2. The claimant's limitations are most important in this step

a. Medical opinion forms are helpful in supporting a claimant's testimony regarding what they are not able to do based on their conditions.

3. The Judge/adjudicator considers

a. Physical abilities- sitting, standing, lifting carrying

b. Mental abilities - the ability to carry out, remember, and understand instructions

c. other abilities - vision, hearing, epilepsy

e. Unable to perform other work and Medical-Vocational Guidelines

1. Once a claimant is unable to perform past relevant work the adjudicator then considers if the claimant can adjust to

work other types of jobs in the national economy.

2. The adjudicator will consider the claimant's RFC, age, education, and work experience.

3. There are five types of jobs

   a. sedentary

   b. light

   c. medium

   d. heavy

   e. very heavy

WHEN SHOULD I APPLY FOR SOCIAL SECURITY DISABILITY?

Sometimes, a particular event can cause someone to be unable to work. Other times, the client has a condition that slowly worsens until the pain becomes unbearable. A person may try to remain at work, but every day is a struggle. Many of our clients who have significant injuries will not be able to work again. Therefore, even if the client disagrees, we have to persuade them to file a claim for disability benefits.

In most cases, there is almost zero risk to applying. If you are unsure if you can return to work due to an injury, then apply for disability benefits now. The process can be long since there are timelines that must be followed, but the sooner you apply, the sooner you can you should receive benefits.

Failing to apply right away could result in either a complete denial of benefits or affect and possibly lower the total amount you receive.

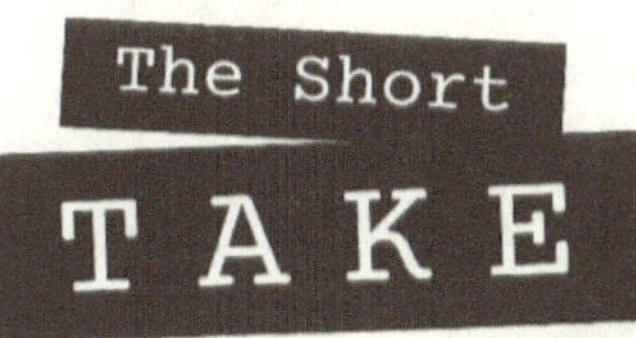

01 Medical Records

Start by collecting your medical records, including any documentation related to you military service, illnesses, injuries, and treatments. This information can be helpful in building a case for your disability claim.

02 File a Claim

To apply for disability benefits, you will need to give a claim with the Veterans Benefits Administration (VBA) of the Department of Veterans Affairs (VA). You can submit your claim online, by mail, or in person at a VA regional office.

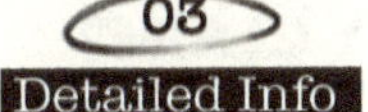

03 Detailed Info

When submitting your claim, provide as much information as possible about your illness or disease, including when you first noticed symptoms, how it has affected your life, and how you believe it is connected to your military service.

04 Medical Evaluation

Get an independent medical evaluation: You may want to consider getting an independent medical evaluation from a doctor who is not affiliated with the VA to provide affections evidence to support your claim.

05 Get a Partner

If you are struggling to navigate the claims process or have concerns about the outcome of your claim, consider working with a VA-accredited attorney or representative. They can help you understand your legal rights and options, and assist you with gathering evidence and presenting your case.

06 Be Patient

The VA disability claims process can take time, so be patient and persistent. Stay informed about the status of your claim, follow up with the VA regularly, and continue to provide any additional information or evidence that may be requested.

WHY TIME IS OF THE ESSENCE

The Disability Determination Services are federally-funded State agencies that determine whether or not an applicant meets medical requirements for disability benefits. Initial claims for disability benefits can take anywhere from three to five months to be decided.

The average Social Security claim lasts 31.6 months

You will receive a letter in the mail that will tell you whether your benefits were approved or denied. If a claimant decides to appeal, then their wait time can be over a year.

Similarly, the VA is overloaded with cases and is not structured to handle all the claims it receives efficiently. They will obtain medical evidence and service records that may assist with analyzing your claim. They may also conduct a C&P (Compensation and Pension) medical examination.

The VA will then issue a Rating Decision, which may explain any award and/or an explanation of their decision.

While most government agencies have gone electronic, the VA still keeps a massive quantity of paper files. The result is a process that typically takes years, but the initial award of benefits sometimes can be surprisingly quick.

The moral of the story? The sooner you put in your claim, the better!

HOW DO I START A SOCIAL SECURITY CLAIM?

To apply now for Social Security benefits, visit www.ssa.gov
To apply now for VA benefits, visit vabenefits.vba.va.gov

1. Initial Application

    a.   To apply for social security disability a claimant must either go to ssa.gov or call toll-free 1-800-772-1213.

    b.   Once the application is received, an adjudicator is assigned the file. During this stage, a claimant may receive a function report, a supplemental pain questionnaire, and a work history report. All forms need to be completed as soon as possible and returned to social security. Additionally, if an adjudicator has attempted to receive information from a claimant and has been unsuccessful, the adjudicator will send a letter informing the claimant that they have 10 days to respond.

    c.   It is important that when a claimant is assigned an adjudicator that the adjudicator's contact information is documented.

    d.   During this stage, it can be helpful to inform the adjudicator of the new medical treatment a claimant has received since the date of application.

        1.   By informing social security of the claimant's medical treatment, social security is on notice to go and get the records.

        2.   This is a cost-effective way of getting records as social security pays for the records saving the client and the firm money in the long run.

    e.   This stage can take anywhere from 1 - 5 months for a decision to be made.

SHOULD I HIRE AN ATTORNEY?

The reasoning is much the same as it is for almost any type of legal matter. The underlying question for most is not what they know, but what a person doesn't know that can trip them up. Expert attorneys handling these types of claims most often know the iceberg under the sea before the ship hits it as opposed to heading for the life rafts after the iceberg was struck and the ship is sinking.

There is a large amount of paperwork and many deadlines involved in applying and/or appealing for disability benefits. Your illness or injury is keeping you from working and earning an income, so do not let your lost wages become a stressful burden by navigating the process alone.

You are not required to hire an attorney. However, a lawyer will make sure that you are given the fair chance you deserve. Lawyers know the right questions to ask and what records are needed to win your case. Far too often clients will think that their case is "simple" or a "slam dunk." Perhaps it should be, but the requirements of disability law may turn a simple case into something much more difficult. What most people do not understand is that when it comes to filing a claim for disability, it is hard to do it right.

Often times what a client believes is important for their case will have no effect on it. Alternatively, something a client thinks is unimportant to their case may be crucial. Understanding the importance of certain factors could make all the difference. An attorney with experience in representing the rights and interests of veterans and disabled persons can help build a strong case to show how much you need compensation for your lost wages.

MEDICAL RECORDS FROM TREATMENT: THE KEY TO YOUR CLAIM

Since disability programs are based upon a person having an injury or illness that renders them incapable to work within the unique rules of each system, the documentation of medical care and treatment for these injuries or illnesses is vital to a successful case. If you are not regularly treated by a doctor, it is entirely possible that even though you cannot work, the documentation is not sufficient enough for the insurance company or the government to agree to receive benefits.

We find that going to the doctor provides invaluable evidence to help your case. Regardless if the doctor does anything for the sick or injured person, the documentation of problems could be the difference in whether you are awarded benefits or not.

The medical records you get from treatment are the key to your claim. They are arguably the most vital and crucial aspect of your disability.

There are a few steps to take to ensure you are efficiently navigating your doctor/client relationship and obtaining the best and most accurate medical records to assist your claim.

- See your doctor regularly and follow his or her recommendations.

- You must secure ongoing medical care. Failure to do so will dramatically decrease your chances of being picked up for Social Security disability.

- If you wish to change medications, consult your doctor–do not switch medications on your own.

- Do not change healthcare providers unless your current provider does not support your application.

- If you have a mental health issue, see a counselor. If possible, try to see a counselor with a Ph.D. or M.D. since Social Security only considers people with these credentials to be acceptable for purposes of a disability application.

Failure to go to a doctor occurs when an injured person does not have health insurance or has lost their health insurance due to illness or injury and cannot afford the premiums. This creates two serious problems because not only will you not get the treatment needed to make you well, but you will not have proper documentation to prove your injuries either. Free clinics, hospitals, and other medical facilities become a lifeline for both care and necessary documentation. In some cases, an injured person may rely on a family member to pay for the doctor's visit with cash, in hopes that the care will help and the documentation will be enough to win a case.

TYPES OF DECISIONS

    a.   Fully Favorable

    b.   Partially Favorable

    c.   Unfavorable

  2. OTR (On the Record)

APPEALING A DENIAL

After you receive a denial letter for disability benefits, you need to notify the Social Security Administration (SSA) that you would like to file a Request for Reconsideration. You or an attorney can do this by completing and sending Form SSA-561-U2 back to the SSA's offices. You have 60 days from the date you received your denial letter to appeal the decision. If you do not appeal the decision within 60 days, you will need to reapply for disability benefits.

The appeals process can take a long time. There are four stages in appealing a denied disability claim, but if you are successful at any of them, the process stops. The first step, a

Request for Reconsideration, can take up to a year if the SSA requires you to get more medical consultations and exams.

a. After an initial denial a claimant will request a reconsideration. Hence you enter a request for reconsideration stage.

b. After an initial denial, a claimant has 60 days to appeal the denial.

c. To request a reconsideration a claimant must appeal the decision and submit a disability report appeal or DRA. Both of these will be discussed in detail later.

d. Once an appeal and DRA are received, the applicant is again assigned a different adjudicator.

e. The client may receive a function report, a supplemental pain questionnaire, and a work history report. Claimants should know that even if they filled it out before they must fill it out again. It is an opportunity to update the new adjudicator on any changes in their condition. Additionally, a third-party individual who the claimant has identified as having knowledge of the claimant's condition may receive a third-party function report. It is again vital that this form is filled out and returned to social security.

1. The key to any of these forms is to assure the client that they should be

as detailed as possible as to the limitations that result from their condition.

2. The claimant should not take this
opportunity to discuss and highlight
all the things they can do.

3. Furthermore, when discussing restrictions on these forms claimants
should always be detailed. For example: if a claimant has spinal stenosis
in their lumbar spine that affects
their ability to sit. A good response
is my back pain affects my ability to
sit. I can sit for a maximum of 15
minutes before I will need to stand,
change positions, or lie down.

4. A bad response is stating they can't
sit for too long. It's too vague and not
very helpful for a third party who
knows nothing about you except
what they read in your medical records and on these forms.

f. Again it is important to note who the adjudicator is.

1. By informing an adjudicator of the
claimant's medical treatment puts
social security on notice to get the
claimant's medical records.

g. This stage can take up to several months. The more medical treatment a claimant has the longer the decision process takes.

h. During this stage, a claimant may be sent for a consultative exam or CE. This is an exam with a doctor whose social security pays for the examination. It is important that a claimant makes an appointment. Most times a CE is an opportunity for a claimant to be evaluated for a condition they may not have previously had an opportunity to be evaluated for.

i. Social Security during the request for reconsideration stage tends to do a deeper review of the claimant's file. Social Security may even have their social security doctors evaluate the file.

B. Request for Hearing

1. After denial of the request for reconsideration, the claimant will request a hearing - hence it's called a request for the hearing stage.

2. Claimant again has 60 days to appeal a decision by completing an appeal and a DRA.

3. At this stage, Social Security does not assign an adjudicator. Instead, there may be a Senior analyst.

4. Typically within 60 days the claimant will receive a letter informing the claimant that their request for a hearing was received and that they will be informed at least 20 days before they have a hearing.

5. At this stage a claimant typically waits anywhere from 15 - 18 months and in some places like Jacksonville and Fort Lauderdale closer to 24 months.

6. Note at this stage the file is no longer with a local office and is now with the Office of Disability Adjudication and Review (ODAR). All correspondence regarding a claimant at the request for hearing stage needs to be done with ODAR.

7. The most important thing is for a claimant to CONTINUE TREATING.

8. Typically, 2-3 months before the hearing, ODAR will call the Coye Law Firm to schedule the hearing. Please note that there are major ODAR offices that schedule for closer hearing offices. Therefore, Fort Lauderdale ODAR will call to schedule a hearing for the Melbourne hearing office.

9. Forms received by claimant

    a. 20-Day letter - letter informing claimant that their request for hearing was received and a hearing will be scheduled at least 20 days before the hearing.

b. VTC objection letter - this letter allows a claimant to object to having their hearing by Video.

   1. If a claimant objects it may cause a delay in being scheduled for a hearing. If a VTC becomes available first a claimant will have to wait until a live hearing becomes available.

   2. If a claimant wants to object they should fill out the form and return it to social security.

   3. If a claimant does not object they may still have a live hearing or a VTC hearing. It just becomes a matter of which comes first.

   4. If a claimant does not want to object they just need to store the letter in their file at home.

II. Hearing Process

A. Hearing

1. The hearing is an informal hearing with formal characteristics. It is formal in that a claimant's testimony is taken under oath. It is informal in that it's not adversarial and a claimant has more freedom to speak freely.

2. The hearing ALWAYS takes place at a hearing office near to the claimant's residence. A claim-

ant ALWAYS has to appear at the local hearing
office.

3.	The hearing will last anywhere from 30 - 45
minutes.

4.	Hearings can either be live or by VTC. Either
way the claimant is accompanied by a Coye
Law Firm Attorney who is live with the claimant in the hearing room.

MAXIMIZE YOUR BENEFITS

Disability benefits can create what we call "staying power."
These benefits may be the sole source of income for our clients and their families and getting these benefits allows them
to survive and settle their other claims on their terms, not
because they have run out of money. If you have more than
one case, say, a Workers' Compensation or personal injury
case, a disability case can increase your value. If Social Security says you are eligible for benefits, then you have solid
proof that the accident in your personal injury or Workers'
Comp case caused substantial injuries. These types of cases are highly interlinked, remember the venn diagram from
page 66.

COMBINING VA WITH SOCIAL SECURITY

Receiving benefits from VA does not necessarily exclude you
from the benefits that Social Security offers for wounded veterans. Injured veterans who are unable to work or engage
in substantial gainful activity can receive benefits from both
programs.

The standards for disability used by Social Security
and the VA are very similar; except the VA requires that all

conditions that prevent a Veteran from working must be ser-vice-connected. For this reason, if Social Security finds you "disabled," and the medical reasons for this decision are all service-connected, the VA cannot disregard the Social Se-curity decision. Since Social Security claims typically resolve faster than VA claims, this may help you with your TDIU claim with the VA. A rating from VA is also very helpful for Social Security disability claims.

COMBINING PRIVATE DISABILITY, WORKERS' COMP, AND SOCIAL SECURITY

A common problem with private disability policies is when the disabled person was hurt at work and has an ongoing Workers' Comp claim. There is a danger of settling the Work-ers' Comp case and some signed releases could waive all rights under the terms of the private disability policy. If you are faced with a job injury that may hinder your ability to work again, then all benefits should be considered, including Workers' Comp, Social Security disability, and private long-term disability. Understanding the relationship between Social Security disability, Workers' Comp, and long-term disability is critical in maximizing benefits for the injured person.

Most private disability plans also require that you apply for Social Security disability and some insurance companies will insist that they represent you in this process.

We generally do not find it helpful to let the insurance company represent your Social Security claim because the insurance company has little incentive for you to be accepted by Social Security and receive benefits. If you are found dis-abled by Social Security, then that can impact whether you are found disabled for the private plan. Additional bad news is that if you begin receiving benefits from Social Security, then your benefits from your private plan may be cut by the amount of the Social Security payment. The better plan is to hire a lawyer that understands the intricacies of Social Security disability and private disability insurance.

It is better to file for Social Security disability using an online application as soon as there is some possibility that an injury or illness will hinder your ability to work and last for one year or more. This is a long process that is instrumental in the private disability insurance situation.

The insurance policy terms are governed by state law if it is a private plan or an employer plan offered through a state or local government.

Private disability policies are complex and have many traps for the unwary. You can avoid problems by reviewing options early on.

CHAPTER TEN

9 TIPS TO HELP YOUR DISABILITY CASE

- Go to the doctor. It is helpful, if not critical, for a winning case.

- See if there are Social Security forms for the doctor to complete as they may apply to your medical situation.

- Generally, it is not a good idea to let your disability insurance company hire an advocate to assist you with your Social Security case. They have little incentive for you to win. If you are denied Social Security, they will then usually deny your claim for long-term disability benefits that you paid for at work. If you are accepted for Social Security, then usually your long-term disability policy will reduce your benefits by the amount of your Social Security disability payment. In short, other than it being a long-term disability plan requirement, the advocate is not in it for you.

- If applying for long-term disability, consider hiring legal help to handle the administrative dispute process. Once you exhaust your administrative remedies, then your only option is to file a lawsuit in Federal District Court, which is an expensive and time- consuming proposition. Unfortunately, we often get cases too late in the process that end up costing our clients more.

- If applying for Veterans TDIU benefits, make sure you have also applied for Social Security disability benefits early on. If you were accepted by Social Security disability as disabled because of your service-connected disability, it will have an enormous influence on your VA claim.

- If you have what we refer to as a joint case, a Social Security and long-term disability case, or a Social Security and a Veterans disability case, make sure that the lawyer understands all aspects of both cases. Generally, it is not helpful to use one legal team for one case and another legal team for the other case. The cases should be handled jointly and if two lawyers/two teams are working separately, then there is a higher chance for mistakes to happen.

- Do not miss appointments or meetings. Ask for rides or help from friends and family members if needed. Detrimental issues can occur when an injured person misses a doctor's appointment, legal hearing, or meeting with Social Security and their legal team.

- If you lose your job due to injury or illness, before deciding to turn down COBRA insurance coverage (an insurance program that allows an employee to continue health insurance coverage after leaving employment), discuss your options with a qualified legal team. Believe it or not, there are some situations where paying for health insurance premiums is more essential than paying the mortgage. If you do not pay your mortgage, you might lose your house. If you do not pay your health insurance premium, your health will suffer and you may not have the medical documentation you need when you have a hearing on your disability benefits.

Photo Courtesy of Jay Baker (CC by 2.0)

CHAPTER ELEVEN

DENIED? DON'T GIVE UP YET!

So, you got your rating from the VA and it's not what you expected. Do you have to just accept it and move on? No! The VA has a claims appeals process that very recently has been updated in an attempt to speed up the claim appeal process.

Remember, you need to appeal – DO NOT reapply. It is rarely, if ever, to your advantage to re- apply than appeal. Why? VA claims are payable from the date the claim is received. If you are continuously moving that date forward by reapplying then you are going to receive fewer benefits. Also, the evidence you used in your initial application may not be considered in your re-application.

On February 19, 2019, the VA officially implemented the Appeals Improvement and Modernization Act (AMA). This act completely changed the way a claim is reviewed in an attempt to speed up the claims process. It streamlined the appeal by introducing "lanes" for a claim appeal to follow. While many legacy claims implemented before August 19, 2019, still utilize the old system, anything filed after this date will follow the new, faster (supposedly) system.

The first important aspect of this new system is the Lanes. Currently, the VA uses three to categorize different appeals.

1)   Higher Lever Review Lane

2)   Supplemental Claim Lane

3)   Appeal to the Board Lane

By introducing lanes, the VA streamlines the appeal process. Previously, the Duty to Assist meant a Board would need to gather and receive evidence and re-evaluate claims based on this evidence frequently. This cycle added months to claims and prevented Veterans from receiving their benefits in a timely manner. Through this new system, the VA no longer has a duty to assist in all but the Supplemental Claim Lane, speeding up the entire process.

An important update with AMA is that the VA is now required to make their claims decisions more detailed and clearly worded. This may seem like a small detail, but it helps you and a lawyer if you so choose a higher one to make the best decision regarding your claim.

Now, we will explain each lane in more detail.

CHAPTER TWELVE

HIGHER LEVEL REVIEW LANE

If you've received an unfavorable result on your application and feel there has been some sort of mistake on your claim, you may decide to file a Higher Level Review (HLR).

In other words, it is a request for another VA officer to review your claim because you believe there was a mistake in how your claim was handled.

It is important to note that the VA will not consider any new evidence with your claim in the HLR lane. Instead, you can submit arguments as to why your prevision decision was unfair or improper. These arguments must be specific and you can't just say you didn't like the VA denied you. An example of a proper HLR argument would be if, in the narrative of the decision, it was listed you did not provide medical evidence of an incident, but your Service Records clearly show the incident, that would be a reason to submit for a Higher Level Review.

If you disagree with your VA decision, you have exactly one year from the date on your decision letter to request the VA complete an HLR. This is done by completing VA Form 20-0996. This form can easily be submitted online through your VA health portal or completed on paper and mailed to:

The Department of Veterans Affairs Claims Intake Center
PO Box 4444
Janesville, WI 53547-4444

It's important to note that the AMA Act significantly restricted the HLR process. For example, previously you would have been able to submit evidence and then have a hearing regarding your case. However, the new process does not allow for the submission of any new evidence and the hearing has been reduced to a telephone call with the adjudicator. This means that if you decide to submit an HLR it is vital you take full advantage of the phone call to receive the most favorable decision.

HLR PHONE CALL TIPS

With the HLR lane, there are three potential results.

1) The Claim adjudicator will overturn the decision based on an obvious error.

2) The Claim adjudicator will return the VA claim for correction.

3) The Claim adjudicator will agree with the previous decision and reject the claim.

Overall, the HLR lane is a great option if there is a clear error in your previous decision. It's important to remember that VA claim reviewers are people too, and mistakes can happen. This lane is a great way to check these errors and get you your benefits.

SUPPLEMENTAL CLAIM LANE

If you submit your claim and receive an unfavorable decision but now have new evidence which may support your claim, you should consider filing a Supplemental Claim.

Just like with an HLR, you have one year from the date of your original decision to file a supplemental claim. To start a Supplemental Claim you must submit VA Form 20-0995 Decision Review Request: Supplemental Claim.

Section 3.1 of the AMA defined a supplemental claim as "any complete claim for a VA benefit on an application form prescribed by the Secretary where an initial or supplemental claim for the same or similar benefit on the same or similar basis was previously decided."

Unlike an HLR, a supplemental claim allows you to submit "New and Relevant Evidence." What is New and Relevant Evidence? It is evidence the VA has not seen that clearly demonstrates the original condition has increased in severity or there has been a new diagnosis. There are 4 main types of evidence which can be submitted.

1) Lay Evidence

2) Medical Treatment Records

3) Independent Medical Opinion

4) Service Records/Service Medical Records

It's pretty self-explanatory, but relevant evidence for your case that hasn't been seen by the VA office. The evidence must help prove a fact in your case, and for Supplemental claims, the evidence can also support a theory that wasn't addressed previously in your case.

Previously, the system required you to submit "new and material" evidence. This meant evidence only to prove new facts could be submitted for your claim. The new system allows for more flexibility in the evidence you submit, expediting the review process and increasing your chances of a favorable decision.

The types of evidence you can submit and their impact on your case have already been covered in the evidence section earlier. The evidence reviewal process does not change for supplemental claims.

If you then decide to submit a supplemental claim, you must complete VA Form 20-0995 along with any information that will be beneficial to your claim. If you don't submit new and relevant evidence for your claim, the VA will register the claim as incomplete and not review your claim.

APPEAL TO THE BOARD LANE

An appeal to the board is technically filing a Notice of Disagreement or VA Form 21-0958. In the Code of Federal Regulations, a Notice of Disagreement is defined as:

> "Written communication from a claimant of their representative expressing dissatisfaction or disagreement with an adjudicative determination by the agency of original jurisdiction and a desire to contest the result."

It must be submitted with one of the dates on your claim decision letter. Importantly, this notice can't just be a general disagreement with your decision; you have to explain the specific part of the claim that you are appealing. For example, if you submit a claim for two disabilities, you must cite which disability rating you are contesting. If you fail to identify the specific issues in the claim you disagree with, the board will dismiss your claim.

To submit your Notice of Disagreement, there are a few things to keep in mind. Firstly, it is recommended you include a cover letter stating that you are submitting a Notice of Disagreement. This is a simple addition that just helps prevent confusion and speed up the review process. Secondly, it is almost always beneficial to request a hearing by a decision review officer. While this does take more time, in my professional experience, you receive a more favorable response with this method.

Once you submit your Notice of Disagreement, it will go to one of three docket options.

1) The first Docket Lane is when the appellate board reviews a Notice of Disagreement with no new evidence and no hearing was requested. The board will just re-review your previous evidence and send you a decision

2) The second Docket Lane is when you have submitted new evidence for your claim, but not a request for a hearing.

3) The third and final Docket Lane is when you request a hearing to review either new evidence or review previously submitted evidence. Once the hearing is scheduled, you have 90 days following the hearing to submit new evidence for your claim.

No docket claim has more or less importance than the others. This lane system, similar to the three appeal lanes, is just to improve the speed of the review process.

CHAPTER THIRTEEN

WHAT'S TAKING SO LONG?

This is the question I hear the most from the veterans I represent, and for good reason. The VA is a massive organization with a huge backlog of claims. In fact, at any given time there may be a backlog of 15,000 - 26,000 cases waiting to be processed. In addition to having a ridiculously long waiting list, the VA is also severely understaffed. There are too few people to make the decisions, and while most government agencies have gone electronic, the VA still keeps a massive quantity of paper files. The result is a process that typically takes years. You could even say you're on civilian time!

Remember how your platoon sergeant told you to keep your paperwork because no one else was going to? Well, believe it or not, the Veterans Administration has a duty to assist, even if you don't have your paperwork!

4 THINGS YOU CAN DO TO MOVE YOUR CASE ALONG QUICKER

When it comes down to acting in a timely manner, the VA can be about as useful as chem-light batteries or a left-handed monkey wrench. Unfortunately, there is not a lot you can do to expedite your case.

However, there are five things you can do to make your claim easier to approve.

1. Have Access to a Physician Outside the VA

A good portion of VA claims relate to service connections in dispute. Therefore, it may be helpful to have access to a physician outside of the VA who is willing to offer his or her medical opinion that your condition and resulting treatment is related to the activities and events you experienced during military service, as well as describe your limitations.

2. Collect Nexus Letters

A Nexus Letter is a letter drafted by your doctor after they have examined your military records and medical files in which they state that, based on their medical opinion, it is "as likely as not" that your medical condition is a result of the activities and events you experienced during military service. Nexus letters can aid in proving that your condition is service-connected.

3. Remember the Buddy System and Collect "Buddy Letters"

Witnesses to your condition are helpful to have on your side. Contact the people you served within in the same unit, at the same time, that are aware of the injuries and experiences you are claiming and ask them to write a letter on your behalf stating information they are personally aware of as it pertains to your condition.

Things have changed and some for the better. There was a time when it was virtually impossible to find the people who you served with. Now, thanks to social media, my clients have found people they served with decades ago to help them out in providing service connections.

If you can believe it, my Uncle who served in Vietnam, in the infantry- 11B no less, in the field, was told by the VA that he couldn't prove he was exposed to Agent Orange. He was clearly speaking to a civilian who had absolutely no idea what happened in the field during close-quarter combat. And he told them that: "You have no idea, the stuff was dripping from the trees."

The fact is, Agent Orange was designed to kill foliage and trees to create zones where the enemy was hiding. It was sprayed by aircraft over large areas. But for people like my uncle, before there was a presumption, you had to prove that you were exposed to it. Now, since the Agent Orange Act of 1991, it is assumed that if you served in the Vietnam War from January 9th, 1963 to May 7th, 1975 that certain diseases are presumed caused by that exposure. More details on Agent Orange and other presumptive conditions are explained earlier in the book.

4. *Create an eBenefits Account*

Your eBenefits account will be very useful to you in your VA claim. On your account, you can manage your health records, obtain military information, and submit evidence. You can also check the status of your claim since your eBenefits account will register when a decision is made and what that decision is. Earlier, we reviewed how to create an eBenefits account but we will review it again below.

HOW TO CREATE AN EBENEFITS ACCOUNT

Step 1) Visit eBenefits.va.gov

Step 2) On the main page, click the tab on the top right labeled "Register."

Step 3) Follow the instructions and prompts to create your account. Make sure to write down your password and ID so you don't forget it later.

This is how you create a basic account, which is the first step. However, a basic account does not have much use unless you upgrade to a premium account. If you upgrade to a premium account, you will be able to apply for new claims, access a VA timeline, submit records, and order some necessary medical supplies (such as hearing aid batteries and diabetic socks). After creating a basic account, you will be prompted to upgrade to premium and authenticate your account.

HOW TO AUTHENTICATE YOUR EBENEFITS ACCOUNT

In order to authenticate your account, you will need to answer 5 questions in order to verify your identity. These 5 questions are pulled from the information found in your credit reports. You will have 2 minutes to answer each question, and allowing the timer to run out can prevent you from completing the authentication process. If this happens to you, you may be locked out of your account. Don't worry, you can still verify your account by going into a VA center, VA hospital or VA clinic. Just tell the receptionist that you need to authenticate your eBenefits account and make sure to bring your account name and password.

CHAPTER FOURTEEN

ELEVEN THINGS YOU NEED TO KNOW ABOUT THE VA PROCESS

I get that this is a big book with a lot of confusing information. That's why I created this section with the top ten most important things for YOU to know before you apply. I created this based on my and my worker's experience with VA cases.

1. APPLY ASAP

It is to your advantage to apply for benefits as early as possible. This is important not only because it gets you your benefits faster, but because it can increase your retroactive benefits.

2. MAKE SURE YOU FILE OFFICIALLY

You must file a formal claim for it to be considered. This must be made using an intent to file form for Fully Developed Claims with VA Form 21-0966 or VA Form application 21-526EZ for all other applications.

Before March 24, 2015, the VA would accept "informal" applications. However, the VA is constantly looking for ways to streamline the system to increase the speed applications are reviewed. Now, an informal application will be listed as "incomplete" and could decrease your retroactive payments.

3. RETROACTIVE PAYMENTS

When veterans apply for benefits, many don't realize that if the VA gives you a positive decision, they will give you a lump sum from the first date of your application to the date of your decision. The actual date the VA receives your formal claim (or intent to file) determines the effective date VA uses to determine when your benefit payments begin.

Overall: Start your application sooner rather than later!!

4. MEDICAL RELEASES AND CONTACT INFORMATION

You must identify and provide contact information for medical providers that you feel support your claim and provide signed medical releases so that VA can access the medical evidence.

Google can be your friend if you aren't sure of the contact info– but the VA will not ask Google or anyone else for that matter!

5. CONDITION OF DISCHARGE

The first thing the VA must consider when evaluating your claim is the Condition of Discharge. If you are not honorably discharged for any reason, you are not eligible for VA Benefits.

6. DD-214

Your DD-214 is extremely important in any claim you make and should be included in the documentation you send with your claim. It's not that hard to get a DD214 if you have an online account, but sometimes it is. Always remember to keep your paperwork after service; the military may lose it!

7. NEXUS

A clear relationship between military service or exposure (Nexus) is required for a claim for service connection condition and compensation. If it's not in your records from your time in the military it sometimes requires other proof. Doctors, other professionals, and even lay statements from buddies who served with you are helpful for proving nexus. The more the better!

8. IS IT IN YOUR FILE?

Any claim for a service-connected condition must show that it is the result of military service activity or exposure to treatment for the condition(s) after military service and an ongoing medical or psychological manifestation. If it's not in the medical records or active duty file, then you need to get creative. Think Nexus Statements!

9. FULLY DEVELOPED CLAIMS

If you submit a Fully Developed Claim, the VA can make a decision for you much faster! A Fully Developed Claim would require you to submit all the evidence that the VA would ordinarily have to request when you submit your application. This is a speedy way to receive benefits but it's not advised unless you have a clear presumptive case or disability (A missing limb, for example.)

10. DUTY TO NOTIFY

The VA is obligated to make "every effort " to obtain medical records from Federal "(VA) sources, private sources and Social Security. However, as noted above, you must make the VA aware of the identity, and contact information necessary to obtain the medical information and again, provide signed releases needed for VA to access such documentation. It is against the law for the VA to complete their duty to assist, but it's fairly common. It's important to recognize when the VA failed to complete this because it makes a great argument when you appeal or review.

11. OBLIGATION TO INFORM

The VA has the obligation to inform you of their decision concerning every claim, the evidence considered, and the rationale for their decision. As soon as you receive any information from the VA, make note of it and save the paper. If you are working with a lawyer, call them ASAP.

CHAPTER FIFTEEN

THE DECISION THAT MAKES ALL THE DIFFERENCE

Applying for benefits is a long, complicated process. Our hope is that reading this book will help to clarify some of the confusing processes involved, but we also understand how overwhelming it can be, especially if you try to go at it alone.

This is where hiring a lawyer can help. A good lawyer will have strong knowledge of the process and the ability to navigate the system comfortably. This may allow the process to go quicker and ensure every step is done properly to make sure you are getting the benefits you deserve. In general, the guidance a lawyer can offer you makes the claim less intimidating and the application process a lot smoother.

Of course, hiring a lawyer can be scary. We do not always have the best reputation, and many people are under the impression that your lawyer will end up taking all of your benefits by the end of the process. However, this is not the case for many lawyers. For example, I am paid on contingency. This means I do not get paid unless you do. If you do not receive benefits, you do not owe me or my team a dime and if you do we only get a percentage of what you receive.

Lawyers are here to help you. It's our job to ensure that you get your benefits.

If you have a more complicated case, for example, a psychological claim, or if you know your VA files are missing information, hiring a lawyer may make the difference between receiving a positive result and being denied the benefits you deserve.

There are three things to consider when hiring an attorney:

1)   VA Accreditation

2)   Experience

3)   Reputation VA Accreditation

VA ACCREDITATION

The VA Accreditation is the minimum requirement for a VA Lawyer. Without this, they cannot represent you in a claim with the VA. Most lawyers list this accreditation on their site, but you can also look for it on the VA accreditation site at: https://www.va.gov/ogc/apps/accreditation/index.asp

EXPERIENCE

Experience is vital in a VA lawyer. The more time you spend working with a system, the better you understand it. With a system like the VA, there are a lot of tricks to learn! Check the lawyer's site to see how many years they have been VA Accredited; even better if they served in the military before! You want a lawyer who knows exactly how to score the maximum benefits available to you. Beware of large advertising law firms! The person who works on your claim is the person you need to pay close attention to in terms of their background, qualifications, and expertise. Even in small firms, experience counts.

REPUTATION

It may seem obvious, but always scope out the reputation of a lawyer you're considering for your VA case. Check the law firm's Google reviews to see that they are highly qualified, communicative, and demonstrate compassion for and dedication to their clients.

I would also suggest asking your own buddies if they've used a lawyer for their claim, and how they felt about their attorney. If your friend has a high opinion of their VA lawyer, trust their experience—a personal recommendation from a trusted friend ensures you'll be in good hands.

HOW TO FIND A LAWYER

Well, by reading this book, you just found one! VA law is one of my firm's specialties. Most lawyers in this field work hard to let Veterans know we are here to help them, so a simple Google Search can also direct you to different VA lawyers in your area.

Another good source is NOVA or the National Association of Veterans Advocates. NOVA is a site for VA-accredited attorneys and advocates dedicated to helping veterans get the representation they deserve. You can contact them by phone at (202) 587-5708, or their website at https://www.vetadvocates.org/cpages/about

CHAPTER SIXTEEN

THE SHORT TAKE!

Sometimes when reading books about how to do things, many skip to the back and get the summary. Here are some key areas for you to consider in your journey;

If you are a veteran and suspect that a disease or illness you have contracted was caused by your military service, there are several tips to help you pursue VA disability benefits:

1. Gather your medical records: Start by collecting your medical records, including any documentation related to your military service, illnesses, injuries, and treatments. This information can help build a case for your disability claim.

2. File a claim with the VA: To apply for disability benefits, you will need to file a claim with the Veterans Benefits Administration (VBA) of the Department of Veterans Affairs (VA). You can submit your claim online, by mail, or in person at a VA regional office.

3. Provide detailed information about your illness: When submitting your claim, provide as much information as possible about your illness or disease, including when

you first noticed symptoms, how it has affected your life, and how you believe it is connected to your military service.

4. Get an independent medical evaluation: You may want to consider getting an independent medical evaluation from a doctor who is not affiliated with the VA to provide additional evidence to support your claim.

5. Consider working with a VA-accredited attorney or representative: If you are struggling to navigate the claims process or have concerns about the outcome of your claim, consider working with a VA-accredited attorney or representative. They can help you understand your legal rights and options, and assist you with gathering evidence and presenting your case.

6. Be patient and persistent: The VA disability claims process can take time, so be patient and persistent. Stay informed about the status of your claim, follow up with the VA regularly, and continue to provide any additional information or evidence that may be requested.

Remember, the VA is there to provide assistance and support to veterans who have been injured or made ill as a result of their service. If you are eligible for benefits, it is important to pursue them to ensure that you receive the care and support you need.

ABOUT THE AUTHOR:

Wade Coye is the managing shareholder and founder of Coye Law Firm, an Orlando-based practice with lawyers handling personal injury, Workers' Compensation, insurance, Social Security Disability, and Veterans Disability Claims Coye received his law degree from the University at Buffalo Law School graduating with honors. He holds bar membership in Florida, Michigan, New York, and the District of Columbia and is admitted to the United States District Court for the Middle District of Florida, the United States Court of Appeals for Veterans' Affairs, the Eleventh Circuit Court of Appeals, and the United States Tax Court. He has tried cases to a verdict and handled appeals in state and federal courts.

Wade's background includes campaign and Capitol Hill assignments for two United States members of Congress and active duty in the United States Army, Infantry.

He was an early adopter of computer technology and the Internet, appearing on one of the first national lists of lawyers using the Internet in 1995 having a website at that time making him one of the first 50 law firms in the country to adopt this new and emerging technology. His continued interest in technology led him to develop a custom database for handling client matters. Today he continues this effort by evaluating and implementing the emergence of artificial intelligence and its use in the legal field. He publishes an electronic weekly newsletter and a printed newspaper with a wide distribution.

He has been married to Joan Coye for over three decades and has five children. He is a licensed instrument-rated private pilot and a certified scuba diver.

ACKNOWLEDGMENT

I want to particularly thank my great office team for helping me with this new edition.

In particular, my undergraduate interns, Abigail Ayres, Mirabella Miller, Zoey Young, Madison Thigpen, and Madison Montgomerie, some of which are with me today and others have moved on to complete their legal education. I also want to thank my long-time paralegal David McWilliams who has worked with me on veterans' claims for over a decade. David is an outstanding and dedicated advocate of veterans having worked on injury and disability matters for consumers for nearly 5 decades! And finally, thank you to my family who is always supportive of my many ventures and interests. My wife Joan, who has always been extraordinarily supportive and encouraging in my many ventures, and my children who are now grown and off on their own careers, I still feel their presence when working in my office.

Of course it's tempting to brag a bit about them, but suffice it to say, for many of my clients who knew them as they grew up, each is doing fabulous and I am of course immensely proud of each of them.

Coye Law Firm

Sometimes... You Need Justice

---

730 Vassar St, Suite 300
Orlando, FL 32804

407-648-4940
866-Wade-Coye

COYELAW.COM

WA